What Remains

What Remains

Journeying Beyond Evangelicalism

Benjamin Garrett

RESOURCE *Publications* • Eugene, Oregon

WHAT REMAINS
Journeying Beyond Evangelicalism

Resource Publications
An Imprint of Wipf and Stock Publishers
199 W. 8th Ave., Suite 3
Eugene, OR 97401

www.wipfandstock.com

PAPERBACK ISBN: 978-1-6667-1523-1
HARDCOVER ISBN: 978-1-6667-1524-8
EBOOK ISBN: 978-1-6667-1525-5

SEPTEMBER 27, 2021

For Cameron Scott Clason.

You did the most difficult thing anyone can do:

you became an adult.

We think about you every day.

Contents

Preface | ix

Acknowledgments | xi

Introduction | xiii

Part I: Made to Be

1   Believers: Safety Through Certainty | 3

2   Bleach: Salvation Through Replication | 13

3   Kings: Security Through Control | 26

4   Afraid: Why Evangelicalism "Worked" For Me | 37

Part II: Outside

5   Already Here: Radically Common Grace | 47

6   Marginalia as Text: Who Is at The Center? | 55

7   Becoming Wilderness: Embracing Uncertainty | 64

Bibliography | 73

Preface

WE'VE ALL DONE IT: sat down on the couch and turned on a movie whose action takes place in a haunted house. A couple with kids buys a house and things are good—for a while. Then unnerving things start to happen: noises, movements, visions. While the characters themselves are still in denial, we think to ourselves, "Ok, if *that* happened to me, I would move."

I used to believe that about myself. I used to believe that if some ancient, malevolent force were wreaking havoc in my home, I would be out. Now I'm not so sure. Putting aside the fear of making a poor real estate investment, there is something more fundamental that would keep me in my home. Would I really allow myself to believe that something from the past, something that is not supposed to be a part of my world anymore, can interrupt my present? Would you?

It's so much easier to believe that the footsteps in the hall are the house settling, the scratching on the windows is branches on glass, the late-night laughter is neighbors up too late, that the dishes fell because of wind, that the gashes you find on your stomach when you wake are self-inflicted.

I would prefer to believe all the above rational explanations. In truth, I have chosen to ignore evidence of an actual haunting in my own life, in my own body. Haven't you?

There is one particular haunting to which I spent years relating through "rational" explanations. This "spirit" laid hold of me as a child, well before I could have known its name. It was like my best friend throughout my childhood. It made me feel safe when I was scared, showed me secret things that other people didn't know, and took me on dazzling adventures. Then, quite suddenly, I wanted very little to do with this friend. Any mention of our relationship was accompanied by apologies, qualifications, justifications. Arguments ensued. A philosophy and religion degree and an M.Div. turned my laptop into an Ouiji board as I sought to put this spirit in its rightful place. And yet, here I am again, performing another seance in response to this same spirit's presence.

The spirit still with us now is Evangelicalism. White American Evangelicalism. Given that you have joined us for this sitting, I am guessing you too are feeling his presence. Perhaps, like me, you have wrestled him into a stalemate. Or perhaps you are only now becoming alarmed by his doings, like you would a friend who has begun to seem sinister, eyes leering slightly, affectionate touches lingering just beyond your comfort level. Or perhaps you have put this spirit long behind you. Your relationship is over. Canceled.

Except here you are, so . . . ?

Sorry. That wasn't fair. You didn't come here to give an account of yourself. No, I have summoned *him* to give the account. *He* will confess. *He* will tell us the way he taught us to see the world, the roles that we ought to occupy, and the pleasures which would become ours if we took up those positions. I am going to make *him* tell it, and tell it plain.

And then it'll be my turn.

I have given up on trying to reason with him. I have turned to things more ancient than him ("deeper magic," to quote a lion he knows well). I have been learning from amoebas and nomads. I have heard ancient truths in strange tongues. I have taken flight from the cerebral and into the corporeal and back again. I want to offer you what I have learned from these journeys. I don't offer my journey as the truth. I offer it as it was offered to me: as grace. I hope it brings you life.

Acknowledgments

As I think about whom to thank for this book, a common theme emerges: this book was made possible by people who were willing to accompany me on the journey it describes. These kinds of traveling companions are precious because they were willing to extend care to three different versions of me: before, during, and after the journey. I am deeply grateful to my family—for encouraging me to be voraciously curious, for allowing me to express my ever-developing perspectives, and with whom I am very lucky to be able to sit down regularly for a pleasant meal (not a thing I take for granted). I am thankful for my friends, my colleagues who were my teachers, and my teachers who were my teachers: Adam Borneman, Ben Allward-Theimer, Cynthia Lindner, Dennis Sansom, Dwight Hopkins, Geoff Wright, Holly Duncan, Jeremy Hall, Keith Putt, Marshall Hatch Jr., Matthew Green, Oreon Trickey, and many more. I would also like to thank my editor, Ulrike Guthrie, who "helped my writing to sing." I take full responsibility for passages where my writing mumbles. I owe a special debt of gratitude to Candra Michelle Garrett, my wife, whose incredible openness to the human experience has greatly increased my own ability to see the sacred in all things. She has had to live with a writer, a task which requires no small measure of tolerance for borderline obsessive behaviors.

Introduction

THIS BOOK IS ABOUT A JOURNEY. It is a travel guide of a way into and a way out of White American Evangelicalism. Like any travel guide, it comes with authorial assumptions about what would make for a rewarding trip. Given that we will be exploring some of the most important aspects of human life—God, bodies, power, grace—it is only fair that I be up front about the kind of journey on which I am attempting to lead you and that I say a bit about how I will guide.

First, where are we going? Well, we are going out, and specifically, out of Evangelicalism. Actually, scratch that. I really mean the reverse: We are going in to get Evangelicalism out of us. You see, one of the things I have learned from my evangelical upbringing and my journey of reorienting my relationship with Evangelicalism is that "leaving" is only part of the work.

This is not to minimize the difficulty and pain of leaving. It is for many a traumatic experience both because leavings as such are often devastating but also because of the particular way Evangelicalism often responds to what it considers its wayward children.

With that said, leaving is still only the beginning. For reasons I will explore throughout the book, we must also deal with the ways Evangelicalism has shaped us. The effects of this shaping linger and emerge in surprising ways if they are not tended to directly. We who have left often find ourselves angry, guilty, ashamed, and anxious for seemingly inexplicable reasons. Not knowing where or when these patterns of thought and feelings will emerge, we sometimes lash out defensively at others. Sometimes we take this negativity inwards and believe ourselves to be inadequate. Sometimes we do both. Unless we attend to what remains within us after we have "left," we are in essence accepting this unnecessary suffering.

Despite how difficult this work can be—and it unfortunately amounts to self-surgery without anesthesia—its healing powers are undeniable. When we allow ourselves to be shaped by different kinds of experiences and communities, we connect with our lives in an entirely different way. That is the ultimate destination of this travel guide: a more authentic connection to ourselves, the world, and the divine.

I will be sharing with you the life I have found outside Evangelicalism. I have been graced with experiences, people, and communities that have allowed me to love the world, life, my neighbors, myself, *and* God deeply and in ways I never thought possible. This way is open to you too.

How will we get to this place? Like any travel guide, you have the freedom to start wherever best suits your needs. There are many stops along the way of this journey and you may not need or want to follow the specific itinerary I have laid out. So, allow me to provide a brief snapshot of this guide so you can start your journey from the point that makes the most sense for you.

Part 1 of this book, "Made to Be," is a description of the shaping forces at work in Evangelicalism. It outlines in detail the kind of person Evangelicalism shapes its people to be, why it seeks to create this kind of person, and how it accomplishes this. Part 1 is diagnostic and surgical. If you have ever been to therapy, this part is like the first session, the one where you describe everything that is wrong, cry a lot, wonder why you are doing it, and somehow feel better afterwards.

Chapters 1 to 3 are exercises in cutting. Evangelicalism makes much of its civility, gentility, and "winsomeness." So, it requires precision and determination to see what is happening beneath the surface. What I reveal is not pretty. It will hurt. It will make you angry. If you are still in Evangelical communities, it will make you uncomfortable around those folks. It will also allow you to name power dynamics that you have felt but that are hard to speak about. It will help you identify the origin point of anxieties which keep you up at night and prevent you from being the person you want to be. It will help you heal because you will finally be able to identify the malaise from which you've been suffering.

Chapter 4 is the hinge point both in terms of focus and style. It describes how my challenges and brokenness made Evangelicalism an appealing way of life to me. The stories I share demonstrate why Evangelicalism "worked" for me—and also encouraged me to be an unhealthy person. What might be jarring for you is the change of voice from clinician to memoirist. While the clinician's perspective was useful for the *via negativa* of understanding Evangelicalism's way of forming people, I believe it best to speak from the "I" in the constructive portion of this work. The need for clarity around the location from which one is speaking will become apparent in Chapter 1.

Chapters 5 to 7 make up Part 2 of this travel guide, "Outside." In these chapters you will hear stories of the people, places, and events that provided an alternative way of being to my evangelical formation. Be warned: If you are looking for a systematic worldview to replace the evangelical worldview, these chapters and this book will not do that work. I do not want to be overly critical of the incredibly intelligent people doing that work out of genuine love of God and neighbor, but I am skeptical about that kind of replacement project for reasons that will become quite clear throughout the book.

Instead, I am offering here a set of stories meant to inspire experiments for living out our rootedness in divine love and acceptance. If Evangelicalism is meteorology, studying the movements in the heavens in order to make them predictable, my new tribe and I are storm chasers. We accept the inherent risk of tailing a tornado. We are just as likely to be grasped by its uncontrollable force as we are to make any important contribution to the field. Or, perhaps more accurately, we believe that any discovery worth having is only attained when we arrive at the point where earth is touched by the Finger of God.

What we see at this point of contact is that God loves life: you, me, everyone, all things. God loves life so much that God has always insisted, and continues to insist, that life be enjoyed. God has created nations, ended empires, become flesh, died, gone to Hell, broken out, and undone death in order to unleash the flourishing of all things.

If you believe Evangelicalism is restraining this flourishing, in you or in people about whom you care, and if you believe there is or might be something else out there that can unleash true flourishing, then this journey is for you.

Part I

Made to Be

1

Believers

Safety Through Certainty

OVER THE NEXT FEW CHAPTERS, I am going to borrow others' voices to tell you my story. This might seem strange at first. We imagine that as we spin the narratives of our lives we are speaking largely with our own voices. Perhaps we name a mentor or influence here or there, but overall we tend to think we are the authors of our own tale.

I have come to believe that the ability to tell one's own story is not our default position. It is a hard-won achievement. We come into the world swaddled in the desires of others. Often there is overlap between these desires and our well-being. And yet, each person, community, and institution we encounter is operating with a story about what well-being means, what the world is like, what people should be like. These stories of desire offer invitations for us to participate. They desire our desire and offer us pleasure in exchange. Think back to school with trips to the treasure box as a reward for sitting quietly, or trophies for success in sports, or later a paycheck for a job well done. These pleasures can be so enticing that we learn not to distinguish between our desires and the desire outside of us. We become agents of an external desire, living in someone else's dreams.[1]

There might be moments where we sense a conflict between what *we* want and what *they* want, but in many cases these outer desires and inner desires blur. Until they don't. These moments of divergent desire are a crisis. Maybe we enter adolescence, fight with our family, break up with a partner, or quit a job. Desires diverge and certain pleasures evaporate. Again, this open conflict is the exception. Most of the time we believe our lives will be more bearable if our insides and our outsides cohere.

There are many different names for this process: education, discipleship, spiritual formation, ideological formation, learning to be part of a family, etc. Regardless of what they are called, these efforts seek to create people with certain desires and the beliefs and practices necessary to fulfill those desires. I call this combination of stories, beliefs, practices, and pleasures *a formation process.*

I hope this description of the formation process makes you uncomfortable. Perhaps you are beginning to reflect on some of the desires that have laid hold of your body, your mind, your desires. The first portion of this book is my reflections on the desires that have shaped me.

I enlist Francis Schaeffer[2] to give voice to these desires, particularly through the words in his book *How Should We Then Live? The Rise and Decline of Western Thought and Culture,* along with the words in *Is Your Church Ready?,* a book edited by Ravi Zacharias and Norman Geisler.[3] Taken together, these two texts describe a way to be human and a picture of what human well-being looks like. The kind of life described in these texts, the desires they express, were once my desires. In fact, the formation process laid out

1. I am indebted to adrienne maree brown's *Emergent Strategy* for this imagery.

2. Francis Schaeffer was a theologian in the mid to late 1900s. He was instrumental in the rise of the Moral Majority/Religious Right and in many ways acted as the philosopher of the group.

3. Ravi Zacheria and Norman Geisler represent popular figures in the theological discipline of apologetics whose Evangelical stream was immensely influential on my own formation process.

by these authors was so powerful I took on an internship at Ravi Zacharias International Ministries (RZIM) one summer with the hopes of becoming an apologist like Ravi.[4] Their world was my world.

What kind of world was it? Into what kind of person were they shaping me? And what was so compelling about this way of life? Don't ever let anyone tell you that evangelicals are prudish. They offer a rich menu of pleasures. The first of these pleasures is an incredibly clear picture of being human. It is with this picture that we begin our journey into the kind of life I was offered.

Human beings are believers.[5] Schaeffer puts it this way, "People are unique in the inner life of the mind—what they are in their thought-world determines how they act."[6] There is a direct connection between what people believe and what they choose to do.

Immediately worries emerge. Where do our ideas come from? How can we have the right thoughts? What happens when we don't? What happens when our neighbors don't?

These are the problems Evangelicalism promises to answer. The external world provides us with ideas. Indeed, Schaeffer suggests we get our formative thoughts and beliefs from external forces, "the way a child catches measles."[7] This measles metaphor indirectly carries through the descriptions of the human mind in these texts and implies that the natural state of our mental world is diseased. Ravi warns, "The worldview of the average person is an ad hoc way of approaching every opportunity. There is no seamless way of thinking, and the result is a breakdown of life's meaning at

---

4. In 2021 allegations of sexual abuse committed by Ravi Zacharias were confirmed and I will be discussing how this abuse is a feature of rather than an anomaly in evangelicalism.

5. I am grateful to James K.A. Smith for laying out the subtle but important distinction between humans as thinkers and humans as believers in *Desiring the Kingdom*. Smith, *Desiring the Kingdom*

6. Schaeffer, *How Should We Then Live?* 19.

7. Schaeffer, *How Should We Then Live?*, 20.

its deepest level of need."[8] Schaeffer goes further and postulates that Nietzsche's madness was due to his inability to hold together a meaningful worldview.[9]

Evangelicalism sees the problem as being not just that we are wrong about the world. Ravi says the average person lacks a "seamless way of thinking." The problem people have is not just that their ideas are incorrect but that those ideas are less a professional map and more an ill-fitting puzzle held together by Elmer's Glue. This produces all sorts of doubts, uncertainties, and a lack of direction.[10] And this confusion is not about abstract things: No, we are talking about the most meaningful parts of our lives—things like love, right and wrong, raising children, voting, what to do with our money, and how to treat our friends and enemies. Our ad hoc worldview cannot give us *solid* answers about how to live. We are lost.

Before we move on to Evangelicalism's solution to this problem, allow yourself to feel this lack of direction in life. Recall some of the conversations you've had where you've dived deeply into a crucial topic of the day only to hit a point at which resolution seems impossible, where no conclusion has been reached but there is also nothing else to say. What about your most valuable relationships? Don't you screw up? Don't you hurt people? Isn't there an alarming inevitability to these injuries we cause? Aren't you lost? I am.

There is a way out of this lostness, says Evangelicalism. There is a map. It was written by human hands but ultimately comes from an infallible source. This map is the Bible. The all-knowing, all present, all powerful creator of the universe sees our desperate

8. Zacharias and Geisler, *Is Your Church Ready?*, 36

9. Schaeffer, *How Should We Then Live?*, 180. Friedrich Nietzsche was a late nineteenth-century German philosopher and philologist. He is considered a grandfather to many existentialist and postmodern philosophers. He suffered a mental breakdown (he allegedly intervened when a man was beating a horse on the street and was himself beaten protecting the animal) at the age of forty-five, which left him incapable of independent living up until his death ten years later.

10. Schaeffer, *How Should We Then Live?*, 63.

need for direction, clarity, and certainty and gives us everything we need to know in order to thrive.[11] The Bible is God's Word to us and we can rest secure in its clear description of the world and the way that we ought to live our lives.

This belief doesn't exist in a vacuum. A whole host of practices support it. By attending a private, Christian school from preschool through college, I experienced perhaps more of these practices than most people, but I suspect if you grew up Evangelical at all, you encountered some combination of these activities too: Bible memory verse quizzes, Sword Drills,[12] endless encouragement to read the Bible daily, an unceasing tide of "biblically-based" sermons—and this was just to support the normal, daily life of a Christian. When things were not going well in your life the Bible was especially crucial.

The Bible, say Evangelicals, contains all the answers to the challenges a person could face. The exhortation to read the Bible daily was ramped up during times of struggle or doubt. This was further supported by prayer seeking God's (sometimes) literal voice to speak into the situation.

Crucial to understanding this set of beliefs and practices is belief in the immediacy of God's presence and words. At no point in *How Shall We Then Live?* or *Is Your Church Ready?* do the authors suggest they are *interpreting* Scripture. Instead, they talk about the Bible as if it is a fully transparent rule of life for believers.

Now, I am confident that if you asked, each of these authors would say the Bible does indeed need to be interpreted and they do gesture to this reality. For instance, Schaeffer notes multiple times the various ways that Christianity and its self-understanding came to be polluted by "humanistic elements". Furthermore, in practice I learned about various interpretations of certain controversial texts (Sodom and Gomorrah for example). Indeed, as a senior in high school we were explicitly taught hermeneutics. There are

11. Schaeffer, *How Should We Then Live?*, 84 and 128.

12. Sword Drills are a game in which a teacher gives a reference for a verse in the Bible and students attempt to see who can find the verse in their Bible first.

recognitions throughout Evangelicalism's practices that the Bible can be misunderstood.

At the same time, these function as exceptions that prove the rule that the Bible is clear. Interpretation comes into play when someone needs to be *corrected*. It is almost as if interpretation is something that is done *by* those outside the fold (leading to moral confusion) or *for* those (temporarily or so far) outside the fold (to bring them back to the truth of the Bible). The default state of biblical encounter is one of truth disclosed by God to God's people. To call this into question is in some way to mark yourself as *not one of us*.

In addition to the positive pleasure of security/certainty on offer to us Bible believers, Evangelicalism is profoundly suspicious of people who do not agree with this way of seeing the world. John Guest[13] puts it like this, "The real issue is not intellectual but moral. Those resisting the gospel may use a plethora of intellectual objections to the Christian claims on their lives, but you can pretty much count on it that the apparent intellectual skepticism is a smokescreen to avoid dealing with the immoral lifestyles or ideas they loathe to relinquish or change."[14]

This belief functions in two crucial ways. First, it gives us believers a moral high ground over the skeptic. Skeptics have no legitimate challenge to our beliefs. All they have is empty justifications for their depravity.[15]

The second function is subtler and more self-directed. It positions our own intellectual doubts in the moral field. It creates

13. John Guest is a pastor and theologian. He is the founder of the Coalition of Christian Outreach and was a participant in the Lausanne Committee on World Evangelicalism, and was a board member of the National Association of Evangelicals.

14. See John Guest, "The Church as the Heart and the Soul of Apologetics", in Zacharias and Geisler, *Is Your Church Ready?*, 50.

15. Schaeffer sees the unbeliever in a slightly different way. They have chosen a set of beliefs (worldview) which centers human beings. This leads to sinful actions. An example, "As the more Christian-dominated consensus weakened, the majority of people adopted two impoverished values: *personal peace* and *affluence*. Schaeffer, *How Should We Then Live?*, 205, emphasis his.

the opportunity for self-surveillance, in which we must determine whether our own doubts are legitimate intellectual concerns or are the machinations of a plotting, warped soul. This self-surveillance preserves the integrity of the community, first by discouraging questions for fear of being found out, and second, by regarding as morally inferior or less honest about themselves than us those who are leaving over seemingly rational disagreements.

I fully understand why I *wanted* to believe this. For someone as bookish as myself, a set of beliefs and practices which gave this kind of power to reading was irresistible. Besides, it is hard to over-emphasize the power of believing that God is the ultimate author of the Bible. The feeling of safety that comes from that belief (regardless of what the Bible might say) is hard to put into words. Even when my doubts or confusion did emerge, the internet age made it possible for me to find resources and explanations to maintain the credibility of this picture of the Bible. Entire cottage industries exist around "resolving" biblical difficulties.

This belief that the Bible is the final word on everything that matters for many years wrapped my psyche in a protective shell. After all, I was walking around with the instruction manual to life! Plus, the idea that God loves me so much that he would create such a thing was a constant source of comfort. I knew who I was. I knew what to do.

Those of you who have fully left the Evangelical camp are probably tearing your hair out. The objections to the above picture of the Bible are bouncing in your head like popcorn in a microwave. I too want to offer a critique here but it's perhaps not the one you are expecting. Remember, I am done trying to reason with Evangelicals about any of this. I will not be trotting out the documentary hypothesis, postmodern hermeneutics or epistemology. There will be no discussion about the age of the earth. I want to go deeper.

The problem with how Evangelicals imagine humans, the problems of being human, and the Bible as a solution to that problem is not that it's factually wrong. To go down that road is to agree with the way Evangelicals see the world. To fight this fight at the level of facts is to agree that human beings are fundamentally believers and what we need most desperately is the correct set of beliefs to guide us through life. This is a fight about certainty. You are staking human well-being on the ability to be *right*. That way lies death. To take the desire for safety and aim it at certainty is to go down a road that will strip you of your humanity.[16]

To offer an example of such Evangelical thinking I turn again to *Is Your Church Ready?*. In it, J. Budziszewski writes:

> Faith means continuing to believe and trust the promises of God, even when the feelings of trust have faltered; God uses the cool seasons of our feelings to exercise us, like a muscle. Hope means fixing our eyes on Heaven even when the feelings of confidence have waned; now we see as in a mirror, darkly, but then we shall see face to face (I Corinthians 13:12). Love means acting for the true good of other persons, even when their hearts desire what poisons their souls and they can only hear the words of love as hate. Sentiment is shifting sand. You can have warm feelings towards God without faith, you can have feelings of optimism without hope, and you can have feelings of sympathy without love. Our God is not sand; he's a Rock.[17]

Notice how Budzieszewski denigrate emotions here. Rather than seeing them as the nerve endings of our being, Budzieszewski consider emotions to be weak and disconnected from reality. He implies that our emotions are not to be trusted, and that we certainly shouldn't heed the emotional signals coming from others.

---

16. To dive more deeply into how this is an obstacle to human flourishing, Dr. Donald Winnicott's brief article *Fear of Breakdown* is worth a read. Winnicott, "Fear of Breakdown," 121–130.

17. See J. Budziszewski, "Off to College: Can We Keep Them?", in Zacharias and Geisler, *Is Your Church Ready?*, 115. J. Budziszewski is a professor of Government and Philosophy at University of Texas at Austin.

Look also at this image of God. "God is not sand: he's a Rock." Never mind that God is also wind, fire, and silence. See how what is prized here is a God who is static and static for us. In the face of our whirlwind of emotions, God stands like an obelisk. Note the patriarchy and the lack of humanity implied here.

In the above quotation Budziszewski brings up mirrors, so let's talk about them. Specifically, let's talk about Jacques Lacan.[18] In one of his seminal essays, Lacan begins by asking us to imagine a baby sitting in front of a mirror. That baby knows itself to be similar to how Budziszewski describes our emotions: erratic, messy, ungainly. It experiences itself as a hot mess. Yet the baby that the baby sees in the mirror is whole. The baby knows that the mirror baby is both itself and not itself. It aspires to be that whole, contained baby, but it knows deep down that it is a vulnerable, permeable, blob of solids and fluids. This desire for wholeness and its immediate thwarting by reality permeates our entire being, says Lacan.

Budziszewski's evocation of the Pauline mirror points to this reality. We wish to escape the ceaseless tide of emotional confusion that besets us. We see a vision of the whole in the mirror but know immediately that it is a lie. And yet God stands beyond that break and offers us the stability we seek.

This is why arguing with Evangelicals about what the Bible does or does not do is a futile exercise. The point is not to identify some other source of stability, like science or historical critical methods or atheism. The point is to love the gross baby in the mirror. To love its snot, tears, shit, and all. The implication is that seeking for something beyond that mess devalues our humanity. To imagine that what we require is something by which to escape our emotions, doubts, and our human fallibility is to suggest that we are not enough, that we must somehow be more than human. Yet I

---

18. Jacques Lacan was a twentieth-century French psychoanalyst and professor. He left his mark not only in the field of psychology but also in philosophy, literary theory, film criticism, political philosophy, and others. Much of what I am about to say comes from his essay *The Mirror Stage as Formative of the I Function as Revealed in Psychoanalytic Experience*.

suggest that if God loves us enough to become a baby, perhaps we could imagine that what we see in the mirror is enough.

As we shall see in the next chapter, the fact that Evangelicals are not in touch with their own "enough-ness" creates tremendous problems for how they view themselves and the way they treat the people in their lives.

2

Bleach

Salvation Through Replication

THERE IS A LOT of consternation about how to define Evangelicalism. There is census data, historical arguments, quadrilaterals etc. Careers have been built around identifying, describing, and marshalling these people. One thing that is universally agreed upon is contained in their name. Evangelicals are evangelical. They want to spread the good news.

I want to explore this defining urge.

The desire to convert is a central (if not the central) constellation of beliefs, practices, desires, and pleasures for the formation process we are interrogating. It is the primary means and goal of Evangelical formation. If you have at any point been Evangelical or even encountered Evangelicals, conversion or the desire to convert has undoubtedly left its marks on you.

The evangelical desire also serves as a bridge between the chapter just concluded and the next chapter. It stands between Evangelicalism's imagination about what it means to be an individual human and Evangelicalism's political imagination. Not that these are discrete stages on a linear journey. One does not become an evangelical individual, then an effective evangelist, and then an evangelical political agent. Instead, these various points of emphasis mutually reinforce one another. To a certain extent, to be presented with Evangelicalism's opinion about what humans are like is to be presented with Evangelicalism's political imagination. As will become clear in this chapter, to take on the desire to convert is in many ways to take on the politics and anthropology of Evangelicalism.

This desire to convert: Where does it come from? What does it mean to share the good news? What do we desire when we desire conversion?

The most straightforward answer is not a bad place to start. Thinking back to the certainty offered by the truth of the Bible, the evangelical desire is a compassionate desire to see people accept the truth and experience the security in certainty it provides. In *Is Your Church Ready?* Pastor Peter J. Grant says,

> This lack of certainty can come from intellectual, emotional, spiritual, or volitional issues . . . Doubt can be a form of double-mindedness, always wavering back and forth between belief and unbelief. Most people recognize this as something they want to avoid. The role of apologetics can be to help them address the reasons for their uncertainty and make a decision based on the facts.[1]

People are suffering existentially because of doubts (not to mention the threat of eternal damnation), and so the presentation of the Gospel can provide people with clarity about their lives by putting them in contact with God and God's Word.[2]

1. See Peter J. Grant, "The Priority of Apologetics in the Church," in Zacharias and Geisler, *Is Your Church Ready?*, 63. Apologetics is an aspect of evangelicalism that focuses on answering questions that skeptics or believers raise about the rational validity of the Gospel. Peter J. Grant is a pastor and nonprofit leader, having been the first Pastor at Buckhead Community Church in Atlanta, Georgia (which became Cumberland Community Church and is in my own backyard) and the founder of Prevision Ministries.

2. I must admit I am incredibly loath to refer to the Bible as God's Word. It strikes me as one of the worst errors Evangelicals make as it confuses scripture with Jesus. To mis-name the Bible this way is a powerful component of

The metaphors that Evangelicals use to describe what is happening here include: offering food, introducing a friend, throwing a lifeline etc. Regardless of imagery, it is made clear through conversation, teaching, preaching, ritual, storytelling, prayer, mission trips, books, radio shows, songs, and more that to be a Christian is to share the gospel with people. If you want to be a part of this community, then the evangelical desire must become your desire and the practices of this community practically ensure that it will.

While this literal answer probably provides a sufficient explanation for the evangelical desire, it's not the only thing that is happening in the beliefs and practices which surround evangelism. There are two crucial mental/emotional operations happening here. Neither can be spoken about directly by those who take up the evangelical desire.

The first operation is the way in which the evangelist is mediating God to the potential convert. While few would say this so nakedly, Ravi states, "Every proclamation necessitates anticipating barriers. And it is only when these barriers are removed by the message and the Holy Spirit brings conviction that the heart can cleave to the cross."[3] In other words, the evangelist has a *necessary* intermediary position between an unbeliever and God. This is even clearer when he says, "leaders have a responsibility to remove obstacles in the paths of listeners so that they can get a direct look at the cross and the person of Christ."[4] The evangelist can make it possible for people to have a "direct look" at God.

While Evangelicals are often fairly "low church" types,[5] we have here an incredibly ancient and priestly position. The evangelical desire provides the Evangelical with a picture of themselves as high priests who are uniquely positioned to reveal God to others.

Evangelical formation as it reinforces the cognition-centric anthropology by directing people to a written word-based approach to knowing God.

3. See Ravi Zacharias, "The Four Challenges of Church Leaders," in Zacharias and Geisler, *Is Your Church Ready?*, 29.

4. See Ravi Zacharias, "The Four Challenges of Church Leaders," in Zacharias and Geisler, *Is Your Church Ready?*, 28.

5. "Low church" refers to churches that do not use traditional liturgies and their accompanying ornamentations/accessories.

The pleasure here is intense. We are talking about being the exclusive holder of secret, divine knowledge. To accept the evangelical desire is to place oneself in this position of knowledge holder and knowledge giver. This is a powerful position in which to be!

I was perfectly willing to occupy this position as well. I remember playing basketball with a neighbor in middle school who for some reason asked me to tell them about God. Instead of complying with the request, I asked, "If I tell you, are you willing to change your life?" I took myself to be responsible for discerning who really deserved to hear about God. I "knew" some people didn't really want to know about God and that no amount of information was going to bring them to accept Jesus as Lord. I wanted my neighbor to confront their own rebellion before sharing the truth with them. This ended the conversation.

It didn't take me long to experience fear and guilt around this experience. I worried that I had just ruined my neighbor's one chance at salvation. Had I condemned them to hell? What did that mean for my own soul?

I tell this story not just to show how this position of mediator of the divine makes you into a jerk, though obviously it can. I also want to show how impossible a position this is for a person. It places a cosmic burden on (in this case young) all too human shoulders. We cannot possibly be responsible for mediating God to our fellow human beings. We will be crushed beneath the weight of that task.

Perhaps you have a similar story. You might have friends or acquaintances who in a past life were the focus of your passionate prayers for their conversion. In retrospect, it might be hard to disentangle genuine feelings of friendship (or perhaps romantic desire) from the urge to convert. You would not be alone if your former missionary zeal led to feelings of embarrassment or even shame.[6]

6. These feelings of shame align with a growing understanding of what psychologists call Moral Injury. Moral Injury most often refers to the experience that soldiers have in conflicts where they are ordered to do things which violate their personal morals. This creates a double-bind where the soldier must, by their own lights, commit a wrong. The guilt and shame experienced

It is very important for you to know that you were a young person trying to make your way in the world. You were doing what children do—trying to attract and hold on to the love of the community around you. It is not your fault that this community's desires were not aimed at human wholeness, and it is not your fault that you wanted to be loved and cared for by the adults in your life.

The second operation is the slippage between the Gospel and one's own beliefs and opinions. While most of the time this slippage is not explicit (Evangelicals talk about their beliefs and practices as The Gospel, The Truth) it actually peeks through in Judy Salsbury's contribution to *Is Your Church Ready?*: "My goal is to lovingly move skeptics to my position without them realizing I've done it."[7] I was honestly shocked the first time I read this sentence. Think back to the importance of certainty. Even to suggest there is such a thing as "my position" is to open up the terrible space of interpretation. This is why Evangelicals do not refer to their beliefs as *their* beliefs but rather as The Gospel. It cannot be admitted that I stand on my own two feet. The idea that *my beliefs* might be only that must be disavowed. As Schaeffer says, "If one starts from individual acts rather than with an absolute, what gives any real certainty concerning what is right and what is wrong about an individual action?"[8] We cannot start with our own reason. We have to start from revelation, Scripture, God's Word and let things flow from there, they say.

The collapse of space between my opinion and truth is a crucial component to the evangelical desire. It provides the justification for getting my thoughts out there because I do not believe they are just my (or just my community's) thoughts. This belief is not operative only in evangelism either. It is incredibly useful for ending a relationship ("God is telling me that we need to break

---

around these moral injuries are incredibly painful. Evangelicalism has left many of us with these kinds of moral wounds.

7. See Judy Salsbury, "Creating an Apologetic Environment in the Home," in Zacharias and Geisler, *Is Your Church Ready?*, 94. Judy Salsbury is an author, speaker and the Founder of Logos Presentations.

8. Schaeffer, *How Should We Then Live?*, 55.

up,") for abusing women,[9] and for conquering people, "I claim this land in the name of God." The formational formula of "I have the truth, I can offer it to people," and the unspoken lack of distinction between "the truth" and "I think" is a heady mix. It provides encouragement and a certain kind of cover to attempt to recruit people to my own ends.

There is a common mistake when people attempt to describe this nexus of truth/conversion/pleasure. I hear it most often from exvangelical types, but it is widespread. The mistake is to think about these beliefs and practices as a conspiracy theory.[10] There is a temptation to imagine that people in positions of power are fully aware of their desires and then intentionally choose Evangelicalism as a cover or justification for those desires. This is wrong in two ways.

First, it is wrong because it gives too much ground to the cognitivist picture Evangelicals hold dear. It imagines a straightforward and fully conscious individualistic connection between desire, thought, and action. It does not take into account the porousness of our desires. It is crucial to recognize that our wants are often moving along tracks laid by others. We are also habit oriented creatures. We often learn to perform actions and take them on as habits without justification on the front end. It is only when

9. From Daniel Shellnut and Kate Siliman's *Christianity Today* article detailing the investigative report into Ravi Zacharias' serial abuse of women: "She said Zacharias "made her pray with him to thank God for the 'opportunity' they both received" and, as with other victims, "called her his 'reward' for living a life of service to God," the report says. Zacharias warned the woman—a fellow believer—if she ever spoke out against him, she would be responsible for millions of souls lost when his reputation was damaged." Shellnut and Kate, *Ravi Zacharias Hid.*

10. What follows does not seek to ignore or refute known historical conspiracies which intertwine with Evangelicalism throughout its history. We should not ignore they ways in which Evangelicalism has been deployed on behalf of capitalists against labor, for example (see Johnson, *A Shopkeeper's Millennium*) or on behalf of the Republican party (just Google Paul Weyrich). I do, however, want to lessen our anxiety around these conspiracies. For one thing, the only difference between a conspiracy and a group of people getting together to do something is perspective. Every institution begins as a conspiracy. What matters about conspiracies is how they work.

results are unpleasant or we encounter someone who is from a different community that a justification is required.

Second, my own experience tells me that things are more complex. I never consciously thought to myself, "I want to be in charge and so I will be an Evangelical because its patriarchal beliefs will provide excellent justification for the accrual of increasing amounts of power." Instead, I heard jokes about female political candidates. I heard jokes about the differences between men and women. As we saw above, I was taught to be incredibly suspicious of emotions and also learned that women were more emotional than men. As a young man, all of these things were pleasurable to hear and made it clear that I had all kinds of leadership roles available to me, most importantly "head of the house." My elders encouraged me to take on leadership positions. They encouraged me to cut through emotional arguments with reason.

All of this was excellent training for a little patriarch and misogynist. And yet the desires this training in patriarchy took captive are not pernicious. Who doesn't want to be encouraged by the adults in their life? Who doesn't want to belong to a community by laughing with friends? Who doesn't want their intellect to be praised? My evangelical formation was not a cover-up of my perverse desires; it was a directing of my human desires towards perverse ends.

None of this is an excuse for any harm I might have caused. I am responsible for the jokes I told, the arguments I made, and my participation in practices that denigrated the people around me. I sinned. In order to move forward I do not require an excuse. I require an explanation. What is so vital to understand about my experience, about the Evangelical experience, about the experience of being a part of any formation process is *how it works*. What kind of people does this system produce, how does it produce them, and what are the consequences of the production for the people produced and the world?[11]

---

11. These are essentially my guiding methodological questions for my interrogation of Evangelicalism. I am intellectually indebted to Michele Foucault's *The Archeology of Knowledge*, Rene Girard's *The Scapegoat* and Mary

Let's answer these questions about Evangelicals. Evangelicals are trying to produce people who make other Evangelicals. This is deranged. Not because there is something particularly wrong with Evangelicals but because this reason for being is the reason for being of cancer. Any formation process which is aiming at pure replication, which seeks to clone, which seeks to eradicate difference, is deranged.[12]

We must speak here of the Evangelical obsession with purity. The normal focus of the purity conversation is sexual. I want to zoom out from this focus by suggesting that Evangelical's obsession with sexual purity (at least for youth, personal sexual ethics disappears from the discourse once they enter adulthood, where the sexual focus shifts to LGTBQ persons) is only a subspecies of a broader desire for purity broadly construed.

For the Evangelical imagination there is truth and untruth. As we have already seen, Evangelicals believe they alone possess the truth. As we have also seen, Evangelicals insist that doubts and resistance come from a combination of selfish desires and human-centric beliefs. We have also observed how this combination of beliefs creates an inquisitorial position that the Evangelical can occupy. When dealing with doubts, Evangelicals believe they can and must discern the motives and worldview operating beneath the doubts on display.[13]

There are seductive pleasures on offer for this position. First, it allows Christians to feel that, "We know what they know better than they know what they know. That's why even a college-age Christian can learn to call their bluffs."[14] Being able to see the truth about someone that they cannot see about themselves is a delicious feeling.

McClintock Fulkerson's *Places of Redemption* for this way of investigating these texts, practices, beliefs, rituals, and ways of being.

12. Even if that process produces progressive people.

13. I have often seen what this paragraph describes remaining true even when people have "left" Evangelicalism.

14. See Dean C. Halverson, "Issues and Approaches Working with Internationals", in Zacharias and Geisler, *Is Your Church Ready?* 122. Dean Halverson is an author, speaker and leader at International Students Inc.

Furthermore, this possession of the truth and this alleged Divine imperative to eradicate falsity is the enabler of a common argumentative practice that I call big game hunting. Big game hunting refers to when an Evangelical picks out an intellectual heavy hitter from the opposite team (Nietzsche was one of Ravi's favorite whipping boys for example), quote a conclusion from this person, and then "demonstrate" how illogical that conclusion is. This is cheap argumentation. Isolating claims without inspecting their grounds is at best lazy and at worst deceptive. However, it allows Evangelicals to *appear* incredibly intelligent. They appear to "own" the libs, the progs, the atheists, and the neo-Marxists.

This tactic is consonant with the Evangelical belief that they are the sole possessors of truth. This allows them not to engage seriously with the arguments of their opponents. Why play the game if you already know the outcome? What really matters is the purity of the Evangelical worldview in the face of the confused, fractured, and just plain wrong opposing worldviews.

In fact, in *Is Your Church Ready?* there is a chapter on proselytizing people from other countries, which encourages Christians to read the religious texts of other religions but to stop or seek Evangelical guidance if these texts raise any doubts about one's own faith.[15] Here again we see the default position of Evangelicals on doubt —that it is bad, dangerous, taboo. Doubt must be contained and eliminated. All this untruth must be removed because it threatens both the eternal soul of the unbeliever but also the certainty which Evangelicals are seeking.

This desire to purify worldviews is not only directed at unbelieving people. John Piper's (in)famous tweet, "Goodbye Rob Bell" after the publication of *Love Wins*[16] is the perfect example of the desire for purity turned inward to the Evangelical community itself. Bell's book attempts to make a case for universal salvation

15. See Dean C. Halverson, "Issues and Approaches Working with Internationals," in Zacharias and Geisler, *Is Your Church Ready?* 146.

16. John Piper is an influential pastor, author, and speaker in the Evangelical world. Rob Bell was also an influential pastor, author, and speaker in the Evangelical world until his 2011 book *Love Wins*, which argued for universalism, put him out of the fold for many other Evangelical leaders.

by adhering closely to the biblical text. From Piper's perspective, this is not worth engaging seriously because it goes against what we already know to be the truth. This justifies removing him from the community.

This desire for purity is unholy. It is unholy because it takes its driving force from an unquenchable anxiety about one's own personal righteousness. It sees different and new ideas as threats to one's own relationship with God. When the possibility of change is seen as a threat, we are dealing with something infernal.[17]

It is unholy, particularly for Gentiles, because it forgets that whatever truth we "have" is only because we have been invited into a story that is older and bigger than our own story. We Gentiles are invited to the story of salvation through the story of Israel. It is because of God's promises to Israel about their relationship to the world that we enter into the Kingdom. We are immigrants in the land of grace.

Furthermore, to speak of truth as possession at all is to misunderstand what is happening. If we look at the trajectory of the disciples in Acts (to which we will return later), they do not have truth as much as they are drowning in the swift moving river of the Spirit's revelation, guidance, and desire.

It is unholy because God does not desire purity. We worship the God-Man. God rips the veil in the temple. God declares the animals clean. God tears down the wall between Jew and Gentile. God's creation is exploding with unnecessary and extravagant difference. Likewise, Jesus flaunts normal conventions of purity. He allows himself to be handled by the impure. Rather than this contact severing his access to grace, grace overwhelms impurity and encircles the polluted, claiming them as part of the beloved community. The desire for purity attempts to paint with bleach where God has painted with a vast array of color.

Now it's time for the people who are still sitting in the Evangelical camp to rip out their hair. What about disciple-making? What about making followers of Jesus, little Christs? Our whole

17. No matter the content.

religion is premised on the reproduction of a single person. We are *Christ's body*, for heaven's sake! Aren't we?

Indeed! But that body is made of many parts! Jesus did not ask the disciples to make people like themselves, but to bring themselves and others into contact with Jesus.

This is what makes the Evangelical slippage between my ideas and the Gospel so dangerous. It deceives us into thinking that our way of being is God's preferred way of being. The evangelical desire to share the truth has wreaked havoc across the centuries because of this blurring of human desire and divine desire.

Particularly egregious is the way in which white Christians have attempted to bleach so much of the world.[18] To trace the history of colonialism is to trace the history of countless confusions between "Thy will be done" and "My will be done." If we really investigate how people's theological imagination operated when it came to conquest, race, and capital, we could never claim with Schaeffer that, "These views were *not* the product of the Christian Consensus, but the churches of that time must be criticized for not shouting loudly enough against these abuses."[19] While most of the time Schaeffer's Christian Consensus is a convenient fiction, colonialism is one of the few places where there was almost a consensus—in favor of domination. As we review the theology of colonizing nations (Catholic or Protestant), we find over and over again people who would come to be regarded as "white" imagining themselves as the sole holders of divine truth. To their minds, this position gave them the *responsibility* to conquer the world in Jesus' name. This is a logical conclusion of the Evangelical desire and it is perhaps the most pleasurable conclusion of all.

The moral obligation to rule the world is the ultimate satisfaction of some of our most profound desires. It allows us to elevate safety against all threats over the people who represent those threats. It allows us to deserve the spoils of this ruling. It allows us

18. The full story of this goes beyond the scope of this book. To get a sweeping, beautifully written, carefully constructed telling of this tragedy you cannot do better than Willie Jennings' *The Christian Imagination.*

19. Schaeffer, *How Should We Then Live?*, 117. Emphasis his.

to maintain an image of righteousness. In short, it allows us to take and take and take and to feel good about doing so. As a process of formation, it allows generations of people to be raised without ever having to wonder whether they might be losing something valuable when they lose their neighbor.

You may have noticed that we have started to talk about topics which would normally be considered political. Shortly I will be turning to speak directly about the Evangelical political imagination. First, I want to summarize quickly how this is linked together now that we have a fuller picture of the connections.

We have discussed the Evangelical picture of human beings as believers. We have identified the way this connects to a desire for stability and certainty. We have seen how the simultaneous need for and possession of certainty creates the impetus for the evangelical desire. We have traced the way in which this evangelical desire is also a desire for purity and leads to the bleaching of the world. Again, this is not actually a linear process. To be invited to align with Evangelical desire is to take on the belief that humans are believers and to go in search of certainty while also to be positioned as one who has the truth. To be one who has the truth is to become bleach because the position of truth-holder contains the imperative to be a truth-sharer. In addition to all the pleasures contained within these beliefs and positions there is the whole practicing community of Evangelicals who encourage, resource, ritualize, practice, and direct each other.

So far, I have spoken very little about the actual *content* of Evangelical beliefs. This is intentional. For those us of who have moved away from an earlier, more conservative Evangelicalism, it is not so much the beliefs that are the source of our haunting, but the formation of a particular way of being. We can expunge all Evangelical content from our minds but still be seeking security through certainty. We needn't read the Bible at all to take on the mission of purification. We don't need to pray daily to be constantly on the hunt for people's secret motives. We have been shaped to be a certain kind of people, to live a certain way. The beliefs are the least of our problems. Discussing the political head on will bring this into sharper relief.

3

Kings

Security Through Control

THIS CHAPTER IS AN EXPERIMENT. I am going to try something here which I am not sure I have seen anyone else try. It may fail completely. I am going to try to talk about (US) Evangelical politics without talking about Republicanism, The Right, The Moral Majority, George Bush, Trump, Reagan, or even something like American Political Conservatism.

It's not that I think these topics are irrelevant, unimportant, or uninteresting. People who are at all interested in politics or religion do well to attend to the unions and divorces of American Evangelicals and American partisan politics.

At the same time, a guiding star for this book is Family Systems Theory, a school of thought within clinical psychology. Family Systems Theory holds that if we are to encourage growth we cannot be overly distracted by what people say at any given time. Instead, we must focus our analytical energy on understanding the larger processes of the systems in which we are caught up. In other words, Family Systems Theory encourages us to focus less on the content of what people say and more on what happens in a particular relational network when certain people say certain things.

Family Systems Theory (especially in the hands of Edwin Friedman) argues that ritualized moments like weddings, baptisms, and funerals are points in our lives at which the processes in which we live (particularly our family systems processes) become particularly visible. I want to zoom in on one such ritual moment to reveal a ritual process that is foundational for the Evangelical political imagination.

The ritual is an underrated genre of sermon called the Jeremiad.[1] A Jeremiad sermon is one in which a prophecy from the Hebrew Bible (from Jeremiah, Isaiah, Joel etc.) is interpreted by way of substituting the contemporary community for Israel as the nation to which the prophecy is directed. The texts often begin with a list of sins (which are read as the contemporary community's sins), details a list of punishments for said sins, and then pivots to the moral commands which can avert said punishments (and are interpreted as the directives for the contemporary community to carry out if they are to avoid destruction). This sermon works on a few different levels, two of which are my focus. First, the sermon enables the community to picture itself as a/the divinely created nation. Second, it makes clear a set of forbidden and necessary behaviors with incredibly high stakes attached. These two features constitute a political imagination because they create a nation, a citizenry, and provide a moral imperative to this citizenry to work for a particular understanding of what is good for the nation. It also places the preacher in the position of the prophet and places his (often his) interpretation (presented as The Truth not merely an interpretation) of the political moment as the divine interpretation.

Schaeffer's *How Should We Then Live?* concludes with a Jeremiad. Perhaps more accurately, *How Should We Then Live?* is a Jeremiad which places its scriptural text at the end. As Schaeffer notes, the title of the book is taken from Ezekiel 33:10. Here is the full text of Ezekiel 33:1–11, 19 which gives the impetus to Schaeffer's Jeremiad:

1. For an in-depth look at this sermon type and for the theory behind what I am going to share, see Sacvan Bercovitch, *The American Jeremiad.*

Again the word of the Lord came unto me, saying,2 Son
of man, speak to the children of thy people, and say unto
them, When I bring the sword upon a land, if the people
of the land take a man of their coasts, and set him for their
watchman:3 If when he seeth the sword come upon the
land, he blow the trumpet, and warn the people;4 Then
whosoever heareth the sound of the trumpet, and taketh
not warning; if the sword come, and take him away, his
blood shall be upon his own head. 5 He heard the sound
of the trumpet, and took not warning; his blood shall
be upon him. But he that taketh warning shall deliver
his soul. 6 But if the watchman see the sword come, and
blow not the trumpet, and the people be not warned; if
the sword come, and take any person from among them,
he is taken away in his iniquity; but his blood will I require at the watchman's hand. 7 So thou, O son of man, I
have set thee a watchman unto the house of Israel; therefore thou shalt hear the word at my mouth, and warn
them from me.8 When I say unto the wicked, O wicked
man, thou shalt surely die; if thou dost not speak to warn
the wicked from his way, that wicked man shall die in
his iniquity; but his blood will I require at thine hand. 9
Nevertheless, if thou warn the wicked of his way to turn
from it; if he do not turn from his way, he shall die in his
iniquity; but thou hast delivered thy soul.10 Therefore, O
thou son of man, speak unto the house of Israel; Thus ye
speak, saying, If our transgressions and our sins be upon
us, and we pine away in them, how should we then live?
11 Say unto them, As I live, saith the Lord God, I have no
pleasure in the death of the wicked; but that the wicked
turn from his way and live: turn ye, turn ye from your
evil ways; for why will ye die, O house of Israel? ...19
But if the wicked turn from his wickedness, and do that
which is lawful and right, he shall live thereby.[2]

I include the full text because it is loaded with identify-forming
and imagination-shaping power when deployed this way.

2. Schaeffer, *How Should We Then Live?*, 257–58.

The first sentence alone fires our imaginations and our pleasure receptors. By placing this at the end of a book full of warnings,
Schaeffer is putting himself in the position of the one to whom
the LORD comes with the command to speak. According to the
subtitle, "The Rise and Decline of Western Thought and Culture,"
Schaeffer's book is his warning to the people of his land. Schaeffer
himself is the watchman/prophet.

Schaeffer shares a tale of Roman decline, Christian ascension,
incursion of Greek philosophical humanism into "pure Christianity," the rise of a human-centric worldview out of this bastard
Christianity, its cultural dominance, and its loss of meaning/truth/
morals leading to a cultural/political vacuum that cries out for an
authoritarian government to provide stability in the absence of
an absolute moral center. In this story, the wicked are humanistic
philosophers and their followers. The judgment coming from the
LORD is an authoritarian regime. That, however, is not the only
judgment in the text. The very soul of the watchman hangs in the
balance. If the watchman does not share the warning of the LORD
to the wicked in the land, then the LORD will hold the watchman
responsible for the blood of the wicked. The watchman saves his
own soul by sharing the warning with the wicked of their land.

What land? The text says Israel. And yet by placing the text
here at the end of a book about "The Rise and Decline of Western
Thought and Culture" Schaeffer has substituted "The West"[3] for
Israel. This is an example of the dangerous gentile substitution
which we mentioned earlier and which Willie Jennings shows in
The Christian Imagination is at the root of so much global blood-
shed throughout history. Yet, for Schaeffer, the West is the inheri-
tor of the Reformation tradition, which to him is the stream of

---

3. This term is fraught. Even in Schaeffer's book he shifts a good deal
between the West as Europe, as Northern Europe, as Northeastern Europe,
Reformation-inspired Europe, Reformation-inspired Europe minus Germany
etc. Perhaps the best way to understand what is meant by the West is to hear
the term as "The white people who agree with my position" = Good Western
Civilization and "The white people who disagree with my position" = Declin-
ing Western Civilization.

Christianity most closely aligned with Scriptural authority and therefore truth.[4]

Where are *we* in this text? What role are *we* offered here? At the risk of being too cheeky: How should *we* then live? Let us remember the evangelical desire and its connection to Evangelical certainty based on the Bible. With these pieces we arrive at a formula pointed to by the Ezekiel text: I have the truth. Therefore, I must share the truth.

What Schaeffer (as an exemplar of Evangelicalism more broadly) is offering us is an interpretation of Western history through the lens of the Bible and which sees history as a progression of ideas. Schaeffer demonstrates a way of telling the story of a civilization by focusing almost exclusively on ideas. Schaeffer does not discuss changing economic conditions, changing political conditions, plagues, famines, wars, technological advancements, or really any other material shift which other ways of doing history would include, emphasize, or center. For Schaeffer, history proceeds by men having ideas and then men implementing those ideas.

As someone who was interested in philosophy, theology, and apologetics, this way of understanding history awakened my interest in the central engine of cultural progress (and also potentially created/increased my interest in these things): The life of the mind was life itself! It also clearly laid out how to be one of the "good guys". As long as my ideas were in line with scripture (as understood by the Evangelical community), I was on the right side of history, I realized.

This meant Evangelicalism not only provided me guidance about my personal life, it also ensured I knew the various trajectories that human history might go and how to participate in human history at the most vital level. All while still in my teens! It would be difficult to overestimate how powerful it is to have such a clear sense of vocation at such a young age. Furthermore, my ability to communicate my understanding of this story with adults and to articulate my role in it led these elders to esteem me. Participating

4. Schaeffer, *How Should We Then Live?*, 80.

in this story allowed me to move towards what seemed like Evangelical adulthood in a context where Evangelical adults could still offer me praise, comfort, and direction. I was allowed to grow up and to feel safe at the same time.

The understanding of adulthood towards which I was moving was obviously not politically neutral. No understanding of adulthood is politically neutral, and so we need to move further into the political assumptions and way of being that guided this formation process.

In Schaeffer's telling there are two ways a nation can go: It can obey God's revelation through Scripture, or it can be human-centric. Countries which obey scripture will be free and thrive, while countries that deny the absolutes in the Bible in favor of a foundation based upon human reason alone will suffer authoritarianism.[5] For Schaeffer, the West has been moving gradually but determinedly towards a human-centric, relativistic culture since the Renaissance. Two focus points of this process for Schaeffer are French Revolution's Reign of Terror and in the (then contemporary) USSR. Schaeffer also sees these tendencies growing in the formerly Reformation based countries,[6] especially in the realms

---

5. Two illustrative quotes: "To whatever degree a society allows the teaching of the Bible to bring forth its natural conclusions, it is able to have form and freedom in society and government." And, "So far in no place have the Communists gained and continued in power, building on their materialistic base, without repressive policies." Schaeffer, *How Should We Then Live?*, 110 & 126, respectively. The second quotation demands particular attention because of the way it whitewashes the history of the supposedly good Reformation-oriented portions of the West. While it is certainly the case that Socialist regimes have come to power through brutal and horrific means, the political and economic formations of the United States and England (Schaeffer's favorite nations as far as intellectual history is concerned) were fueled by both chattel slavery and colonialism. The distinction is really between terror toward one's own citizens versus a more globalized (and longer running) terror. Debating about which of those two is worse strikes me as fruitless.

6. Schaeffer consistently distinguishes between European countries in which Protestantism came to pre-dominate over against countries in which

of journalism, popular culture, and the sciences.[7] As we have already seen, Schaeffer believes authoritarianism is potentially just around the corner.

If we fast forward from the publication of *How Shall We Then Live?* (1976) to *Is Your Church Ready?* (2003) we see that the arguments Schaeffer makes about where our culture is going have become baked into the operating assumptions of these Evangelical intellectuals. Zacharias makes statements like: "As far as the critic is concerned, a careful examination of the cultural mood reveals that it is not just the message of Jesus Christ that has been evicted from reality in this postmodern world of ours, but truth as a category," and "What, therefore, takes place in popular thought is a reflection of the way culture has been *engineered* to deal with truth issues."[8] While Schaeffer doesn't seem to have had the word "postmodernism" at his disposal, he certainly outlined the various strands of thought about which later Evangelicals would use this signifier. By the time I was being recruited into the Evangelical political imagination, it was a given that we were living in a post-truth, postmodern era, and that this context powerfully shapes our mission in the world.

This picture of the world creates a clear, diametric opposition between Evangelicals and society at large. On the one hand you have people who are guided by their own wills, who have more or less succeeded in removing the concept of truth from the culture. On the other hand, you have Christians who are motivated by obedience to God and directed by absolute truth as revealed by God in the Bible. In this worldview, the battle lines are quite clear and it is very rewarding to feel that you are on the right side.

Evangelicals now paint this removal of truth in the form of a conspiracy theory while also denying that they themselves are engaging in conspiracy theorizing. See, for example, the use of the

---

Catholicism maintained its foothold from the 1600s to the 1800s.

7. Schaeffer, *How Should We Then Live?*, 200 and 237.

8. See Zacharias, "The Pastor as Apologist", Zacharias and Geisler, in *Is Your Church Ready?*, 16 and Zacharias, "Four Challenges for Church Leaders," in *Is Your Church Ready?*, 27 (emphasis mine).

word "engineered" in the quotation above from *Is Your Church Ready?* Engineered suggests an engineer but none is named. Rarely do Evangelicals articulate this explicitly as being the work of the devil. Instead, the common image is one of a world gone mad with millions of people duped into believing truth is relative and life has no meaning beyond ourselves, and that Evangelicals alone have a way of being that can lead to happiness and meaning. This way of envisioning the world places the Evangelical in the pleasurable position of a person who is watching a street magician but knows how the trick works while everyone else is mesmerized and clueless.

While all of this might sound fatalistic, it is anything but. There is an incredible amount of work for Evangelicals to do in the cultural and political sphere. In fact, nearly every conversation is loaded with political import. Zacharias, in discussing kitchen table conversations and apologetics states, "Life must move from truth, to experience, to prescription."[9] Read that quote again. In *Is Your Church Ready?* the various authors go to great lengths to argue that apologetical conversations are a *sine qua non* of the Evangelical life, and here we see that their goal is *prescription*. Evangelicals must prescribe, legislate, rule. Whatever particular beliefs Evangelicals have, whatever their particular political policies are, the political imagination of Evangelicals culminates in control. This is the Evangelical vocation: *Control justified by truth in the name of God.*

Yet we must be cautious and not allow ourselves to be suckered into the conspiracy theory story of Evangelicalism. Evangelicals are no more wicked than any other group of people. Nor will we allow Schaeffer's (and others') repeated denials that he is not a theocrat put us completely at ease. Instead, we are going to make clear the particular channel through which Evangelicals are guiding the all too human will to power.

9. See Zacharias, "The Four Challenges for Church Leaders," in Zacharias and Geisler, *Is Your Church Ready?*, 34.

We have been tracking this channel since the first chapter, but we took the scenic route. We began with the human desire for safety, certainty, and belonging. We saw how Evangelicalism provides objects to satisfy these desires through the Bible and a community which embraces those who embrace its particular interpretation of the Bible. Next, we followed this channel as it guided the flow of desire outward. We watched as the desire for certainty and its satisfaction in the Bible necessitates a certain kind of sharing. This sharing is less about giving someone else a gift and more about removing differences allegedly in the name of truth. In this outworking of the desire for truth and certainty, Evangelicals become plastic surgeons, removing what is undesirable and implanting new materials to meet a particular standard of beauty. Bodies must be bleached to conform to truth.

Yet, as we have seen, if you live within the safety-certainty-purity nexus you will inevitably be drawn further into the world. The world displays a kaleidoscope of whirling ambiguities, doubts, and insanity at every level. Evangelicals find themselves in this maelstrom holding on to the Word of God. What can they do but demand this madness kneel before the directives of its maker? How could they not say to the storm, "Be still"?

At the same time, we already know this is the way to destruction. This way leads to taking responsibility for the behavior of others, to demanding that others become like us, and eventually to using force, coercion, and violence to shape the world in our own image. This is how we die and take all creation with us.

The logic of this formation process is nearly inescapable, especially in the context of a community that has been moving in this direction for generations. Plus, why escape? There is so much security, meaning, and pleasure here. "Lord to whom shall we go? You have the words of eternal life."[10] And yet, many of us do escape, or simply find ourselves outside the community, or are kicked out. We

10. John 6:68

stand on the bank of the channel, looking at these desires, positions, pleasures, and we recognize that we no longer wish to swim in that stream. We turn from it and begin walking away. Some of us have a particular destination in mind. Others of us are going to find rocks to bring back and throw at the stream. Some of us have no idea where we are going but we know we aren't staying there.

These journeys are very different and it's possible we may set out on one kind of journey and then get side-tracked or simply decide mid-stride to pursue another direction. Regardless of where we go when we have stood up dripping on the bank, we share a common problem. We all learned to swim in that stream and now we have to walk. Our muscles have been shaped by the needs of a swimmer. Our eyes have been trained to see obstacles and ways through a river. Our very breath is shaped by the rhythm of the water. We have not been prepared for this new journey.

Yet the problem is more dire than a simple lack of preparation. We do not leave Evangelicalism a blank slate. Even though we are trying to leave Evangelicalism behind, old habits die hard. Without conscious effort we will find ourselves relying on the movements and patterns of our Evangelical formation. We have been programmed to be in the world in a particular way. Without intentional re-programming, we will simply put our old operating system to use on new problems, and this will frustrate us either with simple failures or repeated, perverse effects.

This problem of formation is why I have spent so much time outlining Evangelicalism in the way I have. It is why I shied away from beliefs and conventional understandings of Evangelical politics. I didn't need to show you what we used to believe. You are already well aware of that. I needed to show you how we lived and why. I needed to make clear the point at which all our journeys begin.

You (and I) needed to see the soul-warping entanglement of the fear-certainty-control-pleasure that shaped us. We needed to understand why and how we hungered for the safety and control of a cohesive worldview. We needed to remember how a community pleasured us into a certain way of being, a certain kind of belonging. We needed to have our current desires and actions interrogated through this lens. As the Russian Proverb says, "Dwell on the past and you'll lose an eye. Forget the past and you'll lose both eyes."

I want to share with you a bit of my journey and the counterformations that have helped me move towards something else, something better. Before I do, we need to make one more stop. I have to excavate one more piece of this formation. This piece is the most personal to me. I need to share the connection point between Evangelicalism and my struggle with mental illness.

4

Afraid

Why Evangelicalism "Worked" For Me

I CAN'T SLEEP. Not just tonight. Every night for weeks. I'm waiting for it to happen again, like it has happened over and over. My mind begins a familiar routine. I visualize my life: college, then job, then marriage, then kids, then retirement, then death, then nothing. The nothing is where I lose control.

My heart races. I become a passenger in my own body as arms and legs flail. My mouth opens in a silent scream. I stand to run away and realize there is nowhere to run from what I fear. I collapse on the ground. I curl into a ball until my breathing slows, until the panic is done with me. I crawl back into bed and hope I will only have one attack tonight. Sometimes I am lucky. Sometimes I'm not.

I have had panic attacks on and off since I was twelve years old. They began not long after I was sitting on the floor of my bedroom considering ramming a knife into my chest. It's strange to explain now why I wanted to do this. It can be hard to put myself back in that kid's head and to empathize fully with this desire. But I can remember why I wanted to die. I was convinced I would never be able to satisfy the adults around me. I felt, at a fundamental level, that this was the point of my existence, and that if I was going to fail at that then there was no point in continuing to live.

One of the grand ironies of my life, one that I still do not fully understand, was that it was precisely the fear of death that kept me from killing myself. Despite my religious upbringing, as I imagined what awaited me on the other side of dying all I could see was senseless, eternal void. This image made me put the knife away and also made me feel ashamed for being alive. Some part of me felt (or feels?) that had I been a true believer, had I actually accepted the truth of the afterlife guaranteed by my faith, I would have been able to kill myself. In a sense, it was my lack of faith that saved my life.

Due to the stigma around mental health issues that persists even today, I need to say that my mental illness (depression, suicidal ideation, anxiety, panic attacks) wasn't anybody's fault. I have an amazing family who were and are supportive of me. When I told my mom about what I was considering doing with that knife, she very gently told me it would be good for me to get help from a professional. She also let me know I would not be the first person in our family to receive that kind of help. I do not believe I had done anything to deserve the pain I was feeling. I simply was and am sick. Some people get physical diseases, some people get mental illnesses, many people get both. We all need doctors. We all deserve help.

It was not long after I started therapy that my panic attacks started. It would be years before I understood where they came from and how to walk myself back from the edge of such panic. Between the age of twelve and seventeen (when they peaked in regularity and intensity) I went on a journey to correct my lack of faith. I reasoned that if my panic attacks were triggered by a fear of death, then proving the existence of the afterlife would make them stop.

I flung myself headlong into the study of apologetics. I consumed book after book, radio show after radio show. Adults around me noticed this consistent desire to validate my faith and, because they did not why I was doing it, praised and encouraged it. I eagerly challenged the questions and criticisms of others, whether by reading *The God Delusion* when it was still hot off the press, or arguing (sometimes with a great deal of snobbery) with my peers at my church, which was slightly more liberal than my school. I even took time out of a family ski trip in Park City to debate with some Latter-Day Saints in their own library. I left no room for doubt because doubt was death.

It wasn't until my second round of therapy during my junior and senior years of high school that I realized I was taking the wrong medicine. Despite having absorbed every argument for God's existence, Jesus' historical veracity, the historicity of the Bible (especially the resurrection), the ridiculousness of atheism, existentialism, postmodernism, Islam, Buddhism, Hinduism, Mormonism (basically every -ism that didn't start with Evangel-), I was still having panic attacks so severe I essentially became an insomniac.

In reflecting on my life with my therapist, it became clear there was almost no connection between my panic attacks and the information with which I had so studiously filled my head. Instead, it seemed that my panic attacks increased commensurate with the stress in my life. My panic attacks were not the result of a lack of faith. They were my body's way of telling me I wasn't caring for myself. Essentially, during the day I was shutting down my fears and anger, and those feelings came roaring back whenever I tried to sleep. Fortunately for me, my therapist was able to see past the literal content of my panic attacks (fear of death) and understand a process that was and is a central feature of many of my life's difficulties: the fear of saying how I really feel, especially when that feeling is "negative."

Understanding this process helped me to see that my panic attacks were not the problem (though they were certainly *a* problem). My panic attacks were like an alarm bell. They alerted me that I was hiding from myself. This reframing prompted me to relate to my panic attacks very differently. It allowed me to say to myself when I felt an attack coming on, "We don't need to do this. What is really going on?" Instead of being anxious about the panic attack itself, I became curious about what anxieties I might be ignoring during the day. I also found that becoming more aware of my emotions during the day and being able to communicate them to myself and others lessened my panic attacks.

Around the same time that I was uncoupling my fear of death from a perceived lack of faith, I began a process which would ultimately lead to me abandon the career path of apologetics, the related desire to be a professor, Evangelical politics, and ultimately a life that was based on certainty.

While it seemed strange at the time, it would be surprising had these changes not taken place. As for many other people, so for me college was a time of questioning long-held assumptions. While it's possible to go through college and leave with all your closely held beliefs intact, I had no desire to do that. I still wanted the truth, and I was willing to go wherever that journey took me. The friends I made were low-key iconoclasts in their own ways. Each of us was wrestling with our pasts and writing our futures one page at a time. I also encountered professors with quite different aims than many of my high school teachers. Rather than being focused on the acquisition and presentation of pre-determined facts, my professors provided us with tools they expected and encouraged us to put to use in novel ways. We were expected to do new things with old ideas. For me, it was exhilarating.

I studied philosophy and found in Socrates, Nietzsche, Kierkegaard, and Ellul kindred spirits. My understanding of Christian history exploded to include people, events, and arguments that were alien to me. I also began to learn about the ways in which historical Christian debates were just as much about power as they were about theology (and how not to be cynical about this reality). I explored religious practices that were not my own (some outside of Christianity).

I recognized that my Evangelical brothers and sisters were both the victims and perpetrators of weaponizing religious language for war. This hit particularly and uncannily close to home as I learned about the recent history of American involvement in the Middle East. I learned that my previously held beliefs about Muslims (aka my Islamophobia) was not a Christian doctrine but a talking point in a warmongering, profit-making propaganda machine.

At the same time, none of this fundamentally dislodged me from the Evangelical way of being I have outlined. All these discoveries were an expression of a search for truth, certainty, safety, and being able to shape the world to my understanding of the truth. I was still fixated on a thoroughly Schaefferean vocation. I believed humans were believers and that if I could find the truth and convince the masses, then I could help save the world. I still wanted to be an apologist, an author, a professor, a radio show host. I just wanted to be more right than the other guys. I somehow got into the University of Chicago Divinity School saying I wanted to be an apologist (this seemed to confuse the various program directors as much as it confused me). It was this experience that began to alter my trajectory. I will be sharing more of that story in the coming chapters but I wanted to emphasize this in-between place I can now recognize as my brief home.

All my talk down-playing content, avoiding deep descriptions of Evangelical positions on God, Scripture, Politics, etc. stems from this experience. I had replaced a tremendous amount of content in my head. I had all kinds of new beliefs. However, the way I understood myself, my neighbors and my world, had shifted very little. I was on a path that was going to lead to just as much pain for me and my neighbors as I had felt before. I was the 1996 film *Romeo + Juliet*. Compared to the original, the characters were better looking and the set was way cooler, but the story is still a tragedy. I was seeking a certainty that life cannot offer and a control of others that is dehumanizing.

I know I am not unique in experiencing this in-between place. In many ways it aligns with Stage 4 Faith as outlined in James W. Fowler's groundbreaking work *Stages of Faith*. This moment in a person's faith journey describes a break with Stage 3 Faith that relies heavily on content, direction, and security from a community. In other words, in Stage 3 a person's faith identity is a mirror of their community's. In many cases a betrayal or rupture occurs which places a person in a new relationship (often antagonistic) to their previous faith community. For me, the total inability of the faith and practice of Evangelicalism to resolve my mental health issues was this rupture. Yet, in the shift to Stage 4, the relationship to the Stage 3 community remains central but is characterized by a negation and/or conflict with the original community. It's like a bad break-up where each member of the couple intentionally dates the other partner's best friend simply to hurt their ex. They are not in love with the new person. They are using the new person to continue the toxic relationship with their ex. For me, I wanted to be the next evolutionary step in apologetics. What had come before me was flawed and needed a serious reboot. I was still defining myself in relation to Evangelicalism.

I have seen this toxicity too many times to count. I experienced it in one of my MDiv field placements. I was in a progressive church that was originally a church planted by an incredibly conservative church. Many (not all) of the folks going to this church held to their progressivism with an evangelical fervor to which I had grown accustomed during my youth. Their judgmentalism and feelings of superiority relative to conservatives were the mirror image of my own beliefs about progressive Christians: they are heretics. Indeed, because of my conservative upbringing and because my wife worked at a conservative Christian College, there were times we felt like we had to perform progressivism to belong in this community.

I have seen this toxicity played out in progressive Christian conferences where the stated goals of certain initiatives is to have something that looks exactly like the conservative thing but with progressive theology: churches, music, sermons, etc. Perhaps the most egregious example of this is intentionally progressive worship music. In many cases it is simply progressive slogans sung over instruments. This kind of work is doubly derivative as much of Evangelicalism's worship forms are themselves intentional derivations of secular forms of gathering. What is needed here is a radical interrogation of what kind of people we are and what kind of people we hope to become.

In many ways, these experiences are the genesis of this book. The world desperately needs people to begin exploring novel expressions of religious beliefs, rituals, practices, and community. As global migration accelerates, as inequality increases, as the center of Christian faith and practice numerically shifts south, as our economy brings ever more diversity into the workplace, we need new ways to be human together. This is a religious project. At the same time, so much of the "newness" in Christianity is reactionary toxicity.

Perhaps you're itching to tell me: "Ben, you are just trying to save the world again. You are just trying to share/force your beliefs with/on others to bring about the future you want." Yes and no. Yes, I am trying to share my experiences and ideas with people. At the same time, no, I am not trying to save you or the world. I am hoping that by sharing my experiences with you, you will save me, or perhaps we will save each other. This book is my attempt to start a conversation whose direction is unknown to me. I do not have the secret, the key, the answer. I firmly believe such a thing does not really exist (which is perhaps the shortest way to express what the first three chapters of this book were really about). However, I believe that with God's help, we might be able to find a way together.

There is another reason why this book is not about saving the world. Namely, this book is about saving myself. When I set out to write this book, I thought it would be helpful to other people. My goal was to write a book that would help people have a healthier relationship with Evangelicalism, especially their own. Fortunately, I have friends who pushed me on this stated purpose. Specifically, they pushed me to define my own relationship to Evangelicalism. When pushed I waffled. I couldn't really bring myself to say that I was either "in" or "out." In one conversation, my friend Matt gently observed, "Based on what you are saying, I don't think you are an Evangelical."

Hearing this sent my heart racing. Remember, I was trying to learn to listen to my body at this stage, and so this required further investigation. Matt leaned into this conversation to ask why I had such a strong response to the idea of no longer identifying as an Evangelical. The response is simple: it feels like a life-or-death issue.

As I said at the beginning of this chapter, for much of my life the goal has been to accumulate the approval of the authority figures in my life: parents, teachers, pastors, coaches, bosses etc. So many of them have given me the approval I was seeking because of my faith. To stop identifying myself with Evangelicalism feels like cutting off my air supply line. And yet, when I read what I wrote it's obvious I am not an Evangelical anymore.

It is clear to me that the kind of life toward which Evangelicalism points, and which it rewards and creates, is not the life I want. It preyed upon and fed my deepest insecurities. It created a feedback loop between my anxiety, my need for approval, and my intellect. The more afraid I was, the more I performed the role of a good Evangelical and the more praise and support I received. Evangelicalism didn't make me ill but it kept me sick.

So, I am saying it here: I am not an Evangelical anymore.

As I write this book, I feel two things simultaneously. I feel the disapproval of the people whose approval was the basis of my self-worth. I am anxious they might read this book and be angry (or worse) disappointed with me. I feel danger. At the same time, I desperately need the practice of taking a stand outside this community. I need to admit to myself and others where I am and to draw support from the ground beneath my own two feet, to find equilibrium myself. I need to self-differentiate from Evangelicalism. It is time to move out of the house.

So, this book is just as much about me as it is about you. It is both a record of my journey outside Evangelicalism and the journey itself. I believe that I by writing it and you by reading it will get to the end more whole.

Part II

Outside

5

Already Here

Radically Common Grace

ALMOST EVERYONE I KNOW experiences God in nature. It is incredibly difficult to look out over a canyon, or stand in a deep wood, or stroll past a field of wildflowers without feeling some nudge of gratitude, wonder, or care. Everything from the intricate articulations of the earthworm to the rushing of clouds across the blue expanse of sky evokes in us the simultaneous feeling of being much too small and also of being held. I have stared up at the night sky, and the slowly swirling vortex of a billion living explosions has made me feel as if I am both nothing and everything.

This feeling, as overwhelming as it is, does not come to me unfiltered. Instead, this deep sense of wonder I experienced through the lens of my Evangelical mind. I saw the majesty of nature as evidence. Evidence that God exists. Evidence of Creation. Evidence that the claims of Christianity were true. Evidence that we were without excuse before the Maker. Wonder became argument. Awe became certainty. Magnificence was reduced to mastery.

This is no longer how I view nature. Now I am struck by its excess, its lack of dependence on me, my incredible dependence on it. I feel connected to it the way a gear must feel in a clock, or perhaps as a leaf feels on a tree. I marvel at its resilience, violence, and fragility. I am amazed at the way this incredible system we call nature sustains us all.

To move from a place of viewing nature as proof of my position to nature as a universal, gifted, extravagant nurturing power was not a straightforward process. In fact, my experience of nature has only shifted as a consequence of an entirely different shift in experiencing the world. This shift was about learning to see God in new ways, places, and people. It was a shift from understanding God as something I held and gave to others to God as always, already, everywhere at work (and play).

While many people and experiences contributed to forming me into this posture of reception, my time with a nonprofit called EIRO, and specifically its Executive Director Holly Duncan, allowed me to turn inklings and hunches about this new way of seeing God and the world into experiments, habits, and systems.

It's rare to meet people who intentionally embody their ideals. On our best days, most of us are lucky to simply not be raging hypocrites. The opportunities to bring our souls, minds, and bodies together are illusive. In my first conversation with Holly I realized I was meeting one of these rare people. Her days are an expression of her faith. To riff on a quote that is near and dear to her heart, her footsteps are prayers.

Holly took this commitment to integration a step further than her own personal piety, and (with her husband Shawn) created EIRO.[1] Here again, her integrity showed through richly. Not only was EIRO's work (connecting churches to community stakeholders and institutions for community development) an extension of her ideals, but the way this work was done was carefully constructed to align to Holly's values. Taking a cue from Dr. King, means and ends were inseparable. This institutionalization of her own formation was a powerful influence on me.

---

1. EIRO is a transliteration of the ancient Greek verb, "to join."

I joined EIRO as my first job out of grad school. I was the first hire and Shawn had taken a position at Focused Community Strategies.[2] At that point, EIRO was exploring ways to sustain itself and scale. Part of my job was to help figure that out. It was a deep-end-no-floaties situation. While Holly always treated me as a peer, it was also obvious to me that she was taking me under her wing from day one.

After treating me to a lovely Thai lunch at a local restaurant (Holly knew the owner because Holly basically knows every owner of every restaurant in her town of Tucker, Georgia) we hopped into Holly's mini-van for a tour of the city. It's hard to overemphasize how important this moment was, how important these kinds of moments are. Over the next couple of hours, I saw Tucker through Holly's eyes. This is a crucial part of any kind of formation. The moment we begin to see the world the way another sees it is the moment we begin to transform. Holly does not see Tucker as (only) an exurb of Atlanta. For Holly, Tucker is a place where God's kingdom is breaking into existence one hope and act of love at a time.

This idea was not new to me in theory. I had believed God was omnipresent for quite some time. Clark Pinnock's *Flame of Love* had expanded this notion of an ever-present God to emphasize the ways that God was also an operative God. Intellectually I had taken on board the principles of Asset Based Community Development (ABCD to its practitioners), chiefly that when we look at a community, we ought to see in the work of a community's people the work of God and not a place in need of our saving power. The Bible too is littered with stories of God already at work where people were not expecting the divine: Melchizedek, the burning bush, Nineveh, Cornelius. This emphasis on Common Grace and ABCD were what made me want to take the job with EIRO in the first place.

What Holly did was offer me opportunity after opportunity to *practice* these beliefs. We began every meeting by thanking God

---

2. Focused Community Strategies is a long-standing and well-respected community development nonprofit in Atlanta, Georgia. Check them out.

for the opportunity to join in what God was already doing. We did the same any time we were getting ready to meet with a community member, be they a pastor, teacher, city councilor, business owner, or nonprofit staff member. After each of these meetings we would discern what we thought we heard about God's work in this community. What was God getting done through these people? How might we join?

Sometimes these questions were incredibly easy to answer. Teachers were teaching kids. Nonprofits and city officials were providing necessary services. Businesses were trying to organize fundraisers for local initiatives. But other times we had to strain to hear beneath poorly planned or poorly (sometimes problematically) communicated ideas to get at what God was up to. Regardless of the ease of this discernment process, what was constant was the re-formation that was taking place in me.

This practice of expectantly listening to what God was doing in the lives of *everyone* and *everywhere* was drastically different from my Evangelical upbringing. Recall that in the Evangelical mind it is only the Evangelical who mediates God to a lost and confused world. There is clear demarcation between who has God and who doesn't. Assuming that God was already at work in *every* conversation with *everyone* regardless of their personal faith commitments was turning my accustomed world upside down.

The practices of EIRO operate with and instill an entirely different set of assumptions. The prayer to be attentive to what God is doing utterly de-centers the pray-er. We are placed in the position of spectators. What's more, we are spectators who cannot fully see the show in front of us. We are asking for God's help to see and understand. Praying this prayer is surrendering narrative control or, more accurately, admitting that we never had control over the narrative in the first place. The Gospel stops being a story we own in order to share and instead becomes a continuously unraveling series of events to which we bear witness, in both senses of that phrase.

This prayer likewise erodes the desire for purity. By asserting that in every meeting we are looking for and expecting to see God's work, we are admitting that things are going to get messy. Each of us is a tangled ball of joy and pain, strength and weakness, life and death. Praying this prayer with other humans was saying that at least part of the mess is God's work. As the parable teaches, it's not our job to sort the wheat from the chaff. Our job is to bear witness.

This prayerful practice also shaped the way that I saw organizations, institutions, cities, and land. The world became alive with God's gracious, insistent, loving work. How to communicate this?

Go look at a tree. Roots burrow through earth seeking sustenance. Capillaries draw nourishment upward from the roots. Leaves absorb light and convert this into energy. The tree constructs layers of bark day after day, year after year, through these nutrients. This happens whether you are looking or not. Recognize these processes are not *for* you. Realize that this tree has existed before you and will exist after you. The tree is a narrative that has nothing to do with you and is intimately intertwined with your story. All of existence, everyone and everything, is like this and it is all a gift. It is all grace.

This practice of training my eyes to see and my ears to hear the movement of common grace has had a powerful effect on me. It makes it impossible for me to write off other people. It turns every encounter with another person into a divine appointment. It suffuses the everyday and the mundane with sacredness. It eradicates the category of "meaningless." Everything, everywhere, everyone matters because God is at work with all.

Holly's training of my senses operated in tandem with another theoretical notion which had begun to work on my identity and way of being in the world. The idea was (known but rarely fully considered) that God, in Jesus, had died on the cross.[3] In the Gos-

---

3. What follows is inspired by Jürgen Moltmann's *The Crucified God*, G.K. Chesterton's *Orthodoxy*, and Eberhard Jüngel's *God's Being is in Becoming*. Jüngel's entry is particularly important because, borrowing from Barth, he argues that because there is no way God is other than what we see in Jesus, God the Son's choosing incarnation is eternal across all time. God has *always* been with

pel stories we are told that God the Father is silent in the face of God the Son's plea to avoid the agony of the cross. We are told that God the Son's body is tortured, and pierced. God the Son experiences God the Father and God the Spirit's absence on the cross. We are told that whatever death is, God the Son experiences it. What this means is that these experiences—God's silence, isolation, betrayal, pain, doubt, and death—are forever a part of who God is. Through God the Son's sacrifice, God has laid claim to these places of absence and made them places of divine presence.

My prior understanding of God's relationship with the world was primarily an image of separation. The classic diagram of a chasm with humans on one side, God on the other and the cross spanning the gap was fully operative in my mind. It was also operative in my body. Other than sports, I was surrounded exclusively by church-going, Bible-believing people for most of my childhood. I lived fully in the Christian bubble and saw the world only through its refracting walls.

The idea that God had become human to the point of death collapsed this notion of inside and outside. It collapsed the notion that humanity was over here and God was over there. If even death has been brought into God's being, then God has no outside. In the chasm picture, God has walked across the bridge to our side and the chasm has vanished. We have a God who is radically *with* us.

Taking on this idea began to gnaw at my sense of vocation. It's hard to hold onto the idea that my job would be to convince people of believing in Christianity because this puts me *between* God and another person. If God is already with us, there is no *between* available. I can only be alongside others, just as God is alongside both of us. We are on a journey with God together.

It is also impossible to take the stance that doubt is a cover for a moral failing when Jesus experiences full-blown God-forsakenness on the cross. Instead, doubt becomes a genuine encounter with God. The expression of doubt becomes prayer. To cry out, "My God, my God, why have you forsaken me?" is to pray the

us.

prayer our Lord taught us. Whatever doubts another person has (or I have) are invitations for God to reveal Godself in our midst.

My understanding of God, myself, my vocation, other people, my whole world obviously shifted in a dramatic way. The simplest way to describe this change is that I was de-centered. My self-understanding as a truth-holder, as a philosopher king, as a priest was broken down. God is no more with me than with anyone else. God is not waiting on me to do God's work. It should also be clear that a reactionary shift to anti-Evangelicalism wasn't really sustainable for me either. If I am fundamentally not the truth holder, then no amount of shifting the content of "the truth" can keep me in that position.

Instead, through the activation of a different imagination and through the gracious repetition of decentering practices I was guided through by Holly, I began to see myself as just a regular ol' human, trying my best. This may sound like a letdown, but I have experienced it as liberation. It is no longer my job to give people the truth. It is no longer my job to save the world. All I have to do is look for God's always present expressions of love and join in. This has made the mundane sacred and made the people around me revelations of God. If God is radically with them, always at work in their lives, if their existence is a sacrament, what else is there to do!?

If I were to try to summarize this process into a set of steps, a self-guided curriculum, I would say this: Listen to people's hopes and fears. Listen to what people hope their life will look like, and try to see God's desire for the well-being of all creation. This can become complicated. People are messy. Our desires are often aimed at objects that cannot satisfy and yet, if we train our eyes and let go of our prejudices, we can hear divine desire guiding people. St. John Chrysostom said, "Find the door to your heart, and you will find that it is the door to the kingdom of God." This is true. It means that if we find the door to the heart of another, we have found the door to the kingdom of God.

PART II: OUTSIDE

As we listen to people's fears, we will hear what is holding people back from wholeness. Sometimes in people's fears we hear they are holding themselves back. Their insecurities and anxieties are preventing them from attaining the life God dreams for them, for all of us. Other times, we will hear in people's fears the way that the outside world is conspiring against them. We might hear about personal betrayals and systemic injustices. Often when we really listen to people's fears we hear a mix of internal and external blockers to flourishing. In all these things we can be assured that God's desire is to remove these obstacles to a full life. Join where you can. This is where life is.

6

Marginalia as Text
Who Is at The Center?

OCCASIONALLY IN OUR CHILDHOOD we are told things that are both true and not true. For example, I was told that the Bible was a sixty-six-book-long love letter to me. This is beautiful. The idea that God would work with dozens of human beings over hundreds of years to ensure I could know God was incredibly reassuring. It connected to the incredibly intimate and personal way people can encounter scripture. It gave an emotional dimension to the sometimes legalistic-feeling imperative to read scripture daily.

This statement is also not true. Two stories illustrate why.

One of the more rewarding experiences of my time in grad school was facilitating a Bible study with folks experiencing homelessness. This was done through a soup kitchen-style ministry and my first night there told me whatever work I was going to be doing would be unlike anything I had ever done before.

My supervisor encouraged me to pick a table with some of the guests and get to know them. I was served some food and picked a seat at a table that already had five people at it. I asked if I could join, and they said yes. This was the last thing they said to me.

For the next hour they bantered, gossiped, planned and joked... without so much as looking at me. I was completely unnecessary. At first I was annoyed. Then I was annoyed at my selfishness for being annoyed. Then I just sat and accepted the fact that I was unnecessary. Despite all the conditioning and previous experiences that communicated to me that "poor" people needed me, I was learning my privilege did not make me special in the eyes of the people I was supposed to help. This was a chastening experience as I thought about how to lead a Bible study at this ministry.

I decided that whatever leading a Bible study was supposed to look like, it couldn't look like me telling folks what the Bible meant. The guests at this ministry heard all day every day from people who looked like me what they were supposed to think and how they were supposed to be living. My efforts would bring little life if I did the same thing but with the Bible. Instead, I decided to ask questions.

I decided to try to read the biblical text for the week (we mostly read through the Gospel of Mark) as if I had never read it before. In so doing, the Bible became very strange. I would zoom in on a word that a character said or a small detail of gesture that the biblical author described. I tried to imagine what it would feel like to see what the text was describing. What are the people in the story feeling? What would I have felt had I been there? Reading the text this way generated dozens of questions to start conversation.

Talking through these questions with the guests was completely engrossing. Each week it felt as if we had walked into the world of Mark's gospel. We reacted together to what we were seeing and hearing. We reflected on how this experience connected to other experiences in our pasts and how it might inform our future. We learned about each other's values and hopes.

A particular memorable conversation happened during our reading of the Gadarene Demoniac story. It is told in three gospels and is a dramatic scene in all three. Essentially, Jesus encounters a man (two men in Matthew) who is possessed by many demons and lives in a graveyard. He lives in a graveyard because the town from which he comes has exiled him there on account of his possession.

He cuts himself, occasionally escapes from the chains that are supposed to hold him, and returns to the town. Jesus asks the demons their name. They respond that they are Legion. Jesus sends them into some pigs who run into the nearby sea. The townspeople come and find drowning pigs and a free man. They promptly run Jesus out of town.

A question I often asked was, "To whom do you relate in this story?" One of the women shared that she related most to the demoniac. This shocked me. I had been hearing this story since childhood and never once identified with the demon possessed man. In fact, in every story involving an exorcism, I had never connected with the possessed. Unlike other biblical characters, it had never occurred to me to consider the interiority of the possessed. Additionally, it seemed unseemly to relate to a demon possessed person. This person had been made an agent of the enemy (the desire for purity inside me was still operating).

Yet this woman's experience with bi-polar disorder and especially the way she was ostracized by her family and friends connected her to the exiled demoniac. She saw herself in this man and saw God's love for her in Jesus' speaking with and liberating him. It made me think about my own struggles with mental illness, to reflect on the way it felt as if I wasn't fully in control of myself, and the ways mental illness can be isolating.

It also prompted me to reflect on the people with whom I had been reading the Bible up to this point: other white, wealthy, conservative Christians. These folks could afford mental health services. These folks were not kicked out of society. They *were* society. Despite their struggles with mental illness, in this story they (I) identified with Jesus: healer, above the noise, righteous. What else were we missing?

West Garfield Park in Chicago is a complicated place. A bustling Irish-Catholic neighborhood until King's assassination led to riots and fires, it is now known as one of the more dangerous neighborhoods in a city infamous for its gun violence.[1] At the same time, there are people and institutions in West Garfield Park that care deeply about this small collection of blocks. There are parents who worry about their children's safety and education. There are business owners who want to provide quality services and employment to their neighbors. There are churches who want to see their friends and family flourishing and who give of their time, money, and care to make it happen.

I was working at one such church, New Mount Pilgrim Missionary Baptist Church, during my last year in grad school. This church had started a nonprofit called Pilgrim Development Corporation (PDC) and I was its first intern. Most days I was also the only white person for a couple of miles in any direction. It was quite an education.

After I had been working with PDC for a few months, I was feeling a complex set of emotions about the work. I felt guilty about the segregation that created and sustained the dangerous aspects of West Garfield Park. I felt guilty about the fact that at the end of the day I could get in my car and drive back to the safer, heavily and privately policed neighborhood of Hyde Park where I lived. I was powerfully aware of my two decades of private schooling (none of which I paid for personally) that made it nearly impossible for me to fall into the level of poverty that was the statistical average there. So, I decided to do what many white people before me have done. I sought black absolution.

I asked Marshall Hatch Jr., school colleague and son of Rev. Dr. Marshall Hatch Sr. pastor of New Mount Pilgrim, to have a chat with me in the office where I worked at the church. Marshall patiently listened (this, along with an incredibly stilling presence, is one of Marshall's great gifts) as I unburdened myself of my various guilts. Then, Marshall did something that I think only truly lucky white people get to experience from a black person. He did not forgive me. Instead, Marshall simply said, "Think about the people who do not get to leave."

1. This narrative about Chicago is also complicated. I will share why shortly.

This rocked me, or perhaps more accurately said, put me in my place. All my guilt and worry, all my fixation about what I might be doing wrong, all my efforts at implicitly asking for Marshall to make me feel better were ways of keeping myself at the center of the story. My guilt was serving no one but myself. I was asking for someone else to make me feel good about myself, asking Marshall to make me feel accepted. There are two problems with this. First, the Good News is that I am already accepted. God said so and lived so and died so and resurrected so. Second, ignoring this truth was taking my focus, energy, and time away from the people I had supposedly shown up to be with. My guilt was keeping me from being present to my neighbors. Like so many white people before me, I had hijacked the narrative from my black brothers and sisters. Marshall's gentle exhortation brought my attention back to where it belonged: "Think about the people who do not get to leave."

My experiences at the soup kitchen and with Marshall taught me a great deal about community, scripture, and attention. These experiences coincided with another learning which I owe to theologians coming out of the liberationist camp. Liberation theologians noticed that the original authors of the Bible were largely oppressed people writing to and for other oppressed people. The people of Israel were at the margins of near-Eastern society. They were often enslaved, exiled, or only minor players on the global stage. If it wasn't for the Bible itself, we probably would know very little about Abraham and his descendants. They do not figure greatly in the stories left behind by the surrounding empires whose records populate so much of our history. Yet, the marginalia that is the people of Israel's story is *the text* from which our Holy Scriptures emerge. God has decided to tell God's story on the outskirts of the world's great empires.

This is a troubling realization for a white American man in the twenty-first century. My story is definitely not on the margins. My interests are upheld by the most powerful military in human history. My preferences are mirrored back to me in nearly every major cultural artefact I see. The government that sets the laws of this country looks almost entirely like me. My vantage point reading the Bible is much less like the early Christian's and much more like a Roman's. There is a way in which the Bible isn't written for me at all.

As alarming as this was for me to realize, it was vital. All the decentering work that had been happening in my life was creating a vacuum. I had learned that I wasn't the center of God's story. I had learned I could not simply substitute my own people or nation for Israel in the biblical narratives. I had learned I was not the possessor of truth. I had learned I ought not to try to shape people to be identical to me or to conform to my will. What did that leave? What was going to be the center?

The Bible at its most fundamental level answers this question. It is a book by oppressed people for oppressed people. It is a book in which the main character (God) goes to war against injustice. God breaks chains, liberates slaves, crumbles empires, heals the sick, exorcises demons, prevents stonings, frees prisoners, opens minds, forgives sins, and wreaks havoc on any form of oppression. God hears the cries of the oppressed and gets to work. If I claim that God of Israel has laid claim to my life, it's clear what I have to do.

All of this is a far cry from my Evangelical formation process. It cuts across any move to make myself, my interpretation of scripture, my experience, or my community, the center. The arc of scripture seems quite uninterested in right belief or the reproduction of right-believers. It lays bare the lie that God is somehow uniquely on the side of Evangelicals or uniquely concerned about the American experiment. Even if white Evangelicals try to cast themselves as liberators, the biblical narrative shows we are late to the party because God has been at work alongside the oppressed the whole time.

Allow me to describe this discovery in a different way.[2] Thinking again about the arc of scripture, God begins God's walk with humanity with one person, then a couple, then a family, then a tribe, then a nation, then all the nations, then all of creation. Throughout the biblical stories, God's people are continuously scandalized by whom God chooses to include in God's sphere of concern: Rahab, a Moabite woman named Ruth, the city of Nineveh, Gomer, the Canaanite woman, the woman with the alabaster jar, the Ethiopian Eunuch, and Cornelius the Roman Centurion. God shows Godself to be promiscuously faithful and faithfully promiscuous. You can count on God always already loving more people than you and your tribe love right now. Whatever wall you are building, whatever limit you are putting on people's humanity, wherever you are saying some people are not worth being treated with full dignity, God is standing on the other side of the wall, with the dehumanized, inviting you to join the people God loves unreservedly.

The temptation here is to turn the above paragraph into a weapon against *them*. In our current political environment it is easy to identify the wall-builders as conservatives. This is understandable. A not insignificant number of our more conservative brothers and sisters literally want to build a big ugly wall to keep our southern brothers and sisters out of the US. At the same time, I am alarmed when my progressive siblings dehumanize these conservative folks. I regularly hear talk of ostracization, silencing, canceling, ignoring, and simply waiting till they die. You might hate conservatives. God doesn't. If the conservatives are the Pharisees, then we are the ones who need to be sneaking out in the middle of the night to answer their questions about how they can be born again. This is not an argument for an existence without boundaries (more on that in the next chapter). It is an argument for recognizing that changing the brand name of your bleach doesn't change its chemical composition. It is an argument to remind us that God loves more people than we do and is dragging us kicking and screaming into the reconciliation of all things.

2. What follows is heavily influenced by Willie Jennings' stunning *Acts* commentary.

You may have noticed a slight change of emphasis from the first way of talking about this new center compared to the second way of talking about it. Namely that at first it seemed that I was talking about centering the marginalized and that subsequently I seemed to be talking about everyone. This is intentional and autobiographical. When I was firmly ensconced in the Evangelical mindset, I claimed to care about everyone. However, I really cared about them only insofar as I could convert them to assuage my own insecurities about being good enough. In learning about how God's story was a story about liberation of oppressed peoples, I learned about all the ways in which people who believed what I believed had not only failed to join God in God's liberating work but had actually rebelled against God and become oppressors. This led me to wonder about how people became oppressors. Much to my surprise, I learned that people become oppressors because they experience themselves as oppressed or in danger.[3] This means that when we are looking at an apparatus of oppression we are actually looking at feedback loops of fear, violence, and oppression. In any given community we can tell who is "at the bottom" and "at the top" and certain people absolutely visit oppression on others. At the same time, the big picture is that all of us are in thrall to oppressive structures.

The New Testament talks about these structures as "the powers and principalities," but today we speak about them as toxic masculinity, systemic racism, late-stage capitalism etc. In each of these cases we know that everyone's humanity, regardless of where they are in the "hierarchy," is being reduced (though not all in the same way or with the same intensity). So, I have become convinced that *everyone* is desperately in need of liberation. None of us is living up to our full potential because all of us are hamstrung by systemic injustices that lie to us about our worth, our goals, and our ways of being. Caring about the oppressed means caring about everyone. Not in the same way and not at the same time, but we

3. The relationship between fear and oppression was the subject of my MDiv thesis.

cannot pretend that there is somebody who is nobody to God (this includes you).

To continue the curriculum I began to outline at the end of the previous chapter, I want to offer another assignment. If the first was to listen for the desires hiding beneath the words of the people in your life in order to discern where God might be working within them, the second is to repeat this at a tribal level. Who does not belong to your tribe? Who is the demon? Who is the enemy? Or to personalize it yet more: Whom do you and your tribe demonize? Who is your enemy? Seek out their desires (from whatever distance feels safe to you). Why do they desire what they desire? Find something that resonates. Remember, they are human just like you. They too are beloved and animated with divine desire, distorted at points, just like you. Thank God for their desire. This desire is the point of possible joining, the point of shared redemption.

7

Becoming Wilderness
Embracing Uncertainty

ZOMBIES ARE EVERYWHERE. They are now a constant feature of our pop culture imagination. They represent many things, the effects of consumerism, emotional deadening, the lurking presence of death itself etc. Two of my favorite entries in the zombie genre are *The Walking Dead* (*TWD*) and *Zombieland*.[1] Tonally, the two stories couldn't be more different. The former is a meditation on the human capacity for violence and the (im)possibility of its restraint under extreme conditions. *Zombieland* suggests that zombies, while dangerous, are kind of funny. It imagines a world where Twinkies and romantic crushes continue to matter deeply to post-apocalyptic humanity. Despite these differences, *TWD* and *Zombieland* are in dialogue with each other about a fundamental human experience: home.[2]

In *TWD*, the characters are constantly seeking to establish a permanent place of safety. Over the course of the show they find,

1. Both entries in the series rock but I will mostly focus on the second film *Zombieland: Double-Tap*.

2. What follows is a reading of these "texts" inspired by Delueze and Guattari's essay *Treatise on Nomadology: The War Machine*, which can be found in *A Thousand Plateaus*.

create, and occupy a variety of walled zones of security. The periods of wandering between homes are shown as a descent into madness, a place in which the constant threat of the undead strips away our heroes' humanity. Only once they are safely housed in "civilization" can they begin to feel safe and become re-civilized. Security is the primary goal. Everything is secondary or deferred until safety is achieved.

The tremendous irony of *TWD* is that as soon as the characters find safety in civilization they are attacked by other "civilizations." These towns view each other as threats to be controlled or eliminated. Despite sharing the common enemy of zombies, these communities engage in war with each other to possess whatever they feel is a sufficient level of resources to maintain themselves. To its credit, the show itself asks hard questions about how different the "good guys" and the "bad guys" really are. Yet the show sides with the main characters and never calls into question the desire for "civilization" itself.

Zombieland takes an entirely different approach. In the first film the characters are not driven by the desire to make a home but rather a quest to find the last remaining Twinkies on earth. While ridiculous, this points to an imagination that envisions a meaning to life where safety is low on the list of goals. The second film takes on the idea of home directly and joyfully deconstructs it.

The film opens with a band of adventurers taking up residence in the White House, aka the ultimate home. There they are completely safe from zombies. Eventually a few of the characters get a bit stir crazy and strike out, leaving the others to decide whether or not to abandon the safety of home to be with their friends. This journey brings them into contact with other people who are trying various ways to make meaning in Zombieland.

Our adventurers do indeed encounter a civilization in Zombieland. Its members are a peaceful group living it up Coachella-style in a vast, seemingly impregnable tower. Without giving too much away, the film's verdict on this civilization is that it leaves its inhabitants entirely unprepared to cope with the realities of their world. The film concludes (spoiler alert!) with our heroes reuniting and hitting the road, and our narrator concluding that family and friends are home.

While perhaps not entirely intentional, *Zombieland* offers a powerful challenge to *TWD*. The film suggests that the insatiable desire for safety and security demonstrated on the show is actually a poor adaptation to a dangerous world. This is not to say our movie heroes imagine that zombies aren't dangerous. On the contrary, the characters have adapted highly sophisticated ways to protect themselves from the undead. However, they do not think safety from the walking dead is an end in itself. They have learned to deal with zombies *on the journey* rather than dealing with them *as* the journey.

Furthermore, the individuals in the group don't all share the same goals. Instead, they organize around individual quests, supporting each other in their personal goals. This is a far cry from the organization we see in *TWD*. In every case the actions of the community are ultimately decided by a leader who wields either violence or charisma (or both) to bring the community towards their determined aims. In *TWD* the ultimate motivator is what will make the community the safest and so fear drives everyone together. In *Zombieland*, life is meant to be meaningful and so people join in what gives them meaning, understanding that there is no ultimate safety net.

If I were to apply these two approaches to the subject of this book, I might identify Evangelicals with *TWD* and suggest that what I am after, or where I am going, is more like the way of being revealed in *Zombieland*.

In order to cope with a dangerous world, Evangelicals, like the protagonists of *TWD*, aim at stability and control. Conformity is highly prized because difference represents a threat to a stable order and it is easy to become suspicious of the morals of the different. Deliberation is possible, but the ultimate value of certainty cannot be questioned without putting you very much on the outside of the community. Expressing difference can get you censured or exiled or (in the case of Muslims in the twenty-first century) killed.

As psychoanalyst Donald Winnicott said, all of this is denial. We are always already living on the other side of the breakdown. This was certainly true of my own life. My Evangelicalism became all-consuming *after* my suicidal ideations. I was trying to prevent future breakdowns by denying that such a breakdown was possible. I was attempting to use Evangelicalism to convince myself that I had nothing of which to be afraid—after I had already met the object of my fear. No amount of telling myself, "I shouldn't be afraid of death because x, y, and z" made it so that I actually wasn't afraid of death.

Living in *Zombieland*, however, takes it for granted that death by zombie is always a possibility, no matter what. This means that safety can never be the ultimate value because it is a mirage. This is a powerful metaphorical critique against the Evangelical way of being. Intellectual certainty about what really matters, in my experience and in the experience of every human I've ever met, is an impossibility. We can always wonder, doubt, fear. These emotions are not bad in themselves. They are simply part of the journey of arriving at a choice. Furthermore, there is nothing wrong with making an important choice and saying, "I'm not certain this is right but it is what I am going to do." Isn't this the reality of the most important choices in our lives? Isn't courage and beauty found precisely where we don't know exactly what we are doing or exactly how it's going to turn out and we commit anyway?

This past year has been the deepest wilderness I have ever walked. Late one evening in February of 2020, my wife and I received a call from the hospital that Cameron, my wife's eighteen-year-old brother, had been in a serious automobile accident. We arrived at the hospital and crammed together in a small waiting room with my mother-in-law and her partner. The doctor arrived and told us that Cameron had died from his injuries shortly after arriving at the hospital. This was the worst moment of all our lives.

Each of us experienced this shock in a different way. For each of us, Cameron's death was a breakdown. A fundamental aspect of our identity (as mother, father, sister, brother, or brother-in-law) had died with Cameron. I remember standing in the hospital, stunned that his death was now a part of my life. Some part of my being still believed in the savior position for which Evangelicalism had shaped me, and that part of me was speechless before the reality that I desperately needed to be rescued in this moment. I had firmly believed that this kind of thing couldn't happen to me. It happened to other people. My role was to help, not suffer.

In the following days, weeks, and months we struggled through this post-breakdown wilderness. In many cases, people joined us in this wilderness. They did not rush our journey or expect us to be anything other than what we were in each moment. They cried when we cried, laughed when we laughed and were silent when no words were possible. This too is the gift my wife and I attempted to offer each other: presence in the wilderness. We had nothing else to give.

Yet there were some people who sought to deny the breakdown. Some attempted to hurry us through the wilderness. They told us that "God has a reason for doing this." I am convinced this is ultimately a self-directed statement. It is the speaker's attempt to deny the breakdown, deny that we are in the wilderness. It is an empty incantation to summon walls of safety in the wilderness.

The Evangelical approach attempts to deny that life is lived in a post-breakdown wilderness.[3] It imagines the possibility of finding an oasis around which to build a city. Going further, it claims already to have found the oasis and have built the city. From the perspective of those in the city, the wilderness is entirely unnecessary. It is for outsiders. Outsiders are allowed in but only if they do not question the rules of the city. In addition, the Evangelical approach uses the threat of the wilderness outside to ensure that order is maintained on the inside. It sees the outside as the domain of the wicked, the unstable, the lost.

Cameron's death has taught me that there is no logic by which we can by live that will keep the breakdown from happening, and

3. I am drawing here from Brené Brown's *Braving the Wilderness* with splashes of Deleuze and Guattari's *A Thousand Plateaus*.

there is no logic we can summon to make the breakdown less horrific. We can only accept that this breakdown is our breakdown and that there are others (including God) who are willing to be with us during it and into the future. I have learned that trying to do more will make you feel like you have less, and accepting this reality gives you more than enough.

I have learned that the wilderness is where God leads God's people to new life. The wilderness is an acceptance of life's ambiguities sustained by God's presence. It is saying, "I love you," first. It is about putting boundaries on a toxic relationship. It is about seeking the perspective of an outsider. It is about taking a stand on your principles. It is about admitting you are wrong, that you hurt someone. It is about forgiving and being forgiven. It is simply about being really, truly, present with another person.

I am not trying to minimize the danger of any of these situations. Some of them can break your heart. Some of them can get you killed.[4] Yet, accepting these risks and acting anyway is where life becomes real. These are the moments in which we grow. These are the moments in which we stop being defined by the systems in which we live and start writing our stories in a different direction.

I also don't want to minimize the loneliness that can accompany this wilderness existence. Refusing to allow yourself to be determined by a community makes belonging tenuous. Being determined by a community means never having to explain yourself, never having to define yourself. To be self-differentiated (Family System Theory's way of saying not determined by the systems or communities we live in) is a continual practice of self-definition. It is to say over and over, "I am here." It is to stand out and be vulnerable. Other people's anxiety will lead them to misunderstand, ignore, or attack you in such situations. It will hurt.

However, there are other people wandering in this wilderness. They will break bread with you. They will sustain you on your

---

4. I also want to acknowledge my privilege when speaking about agency and danger. There is a big difference between choosing danger/pain and having it inflicted upon you. We must be very careful to discern the sources of pain when we make choices or are walking alongside others.

journey. They may even walk a few miles with you and shoulder your pack while they do. My experience has taught me to spend as much time with these folks as I do with anyone else. Self-differentiation is lonely enough without intentionally choosing to be alone or around people who cannot be *with* you.

Find people who see you. Find people who genuinely encourage your flourishing, who invite you to be more fully yourself. Eat with them. Drink with them. Prioritize time with them. They are part of home in the wilderness.

Accepting the wilderness will also change your relationship with church. Individual churches have a hard time remembering in their practices that they are not The Church. In order to survive they have to funnel your time, your attention, and your energy toward themselves. To be self-differentiated with a church is to be able to tell it "yes" *and* "no". The best advice I ever been given in relation to this was from my friend Adam who has been a pastor and working in support of pastors his whole career. He told me, "Decide what you want to get from church and what you are willing to give to church. Then, only do those things." These clear boundaries have allowed me to stay in relationship with my church.

There is something beyond accepting the world as a wilderness. Despite how much bravery it can take to leave our imagined stability and how much practice it takes to learn to live in the wilderness, this is only the beginning.

At this point in the narrative we are coming to the limits of my own experience. While so far I have shared with you from my own life, what comes next is almost purely aspirational for me.

At one point in *Braving the Wilderness*, author Brené Brown suggests one can become a wilderness. This notion sent lightning through me. I had been reading a book called *A Thousand Plateaus* at about the same time and was incredibly intrigued by Gilles Deleuze and Felix Guattari's notion of becomings. Becoming for them is the idea that we might experiment with our lives inspired by another aspect of life. We might become flowers by deciding that sunlight will become an essential part of our daily routine. We might become dogs by exuberantly and ridiculously greeting our friends and loved ones when they enter a room. We might become banshees in prophetically announcing the end of something that has outlived its allotted time. None of these becomings are permanent, nor are they intended to be completed. They are masks, moods, experiments. They are always works in progress.

I was struck by the idea of becoming wilderness. What might this mean? What would a practice of becoming wilderness entail? Perhaps it would look like some of those steps into the wilderness I described earlier. To tell someone you love them is to invite them into a space of uncertainty, a place where boundaries are put into question, and identity has to be reconfigured. Marshall became a wilderness for me when he challenged me to focus my attention on the people of West Garfield Park. Matt became a wilderness for me when he said I didn't sound like an Evangelical.

In each of these cases becoming wilderness is an invitation. It is an invitation to be a place to which someone else wanders outside their comfort zone. It invites them to explore new ways of being. This invitation can come through thoughtful critique or through an unexpected and deep encouragement. It lays bare where someone is defending themselves against a higher good and offers a way forward.

This book has been an attempt at becoming wilderness for me. If you are still at the back gate of the city, I hope it helps you take your first step. If you have been wandering to the point of dehydration and exhaustion, I hope it provides refreshment. If you are a creature of the wilderness, I hope it offers new sights to explore. Wherever you have been or are going, I am happy to have your company. And I hope my company has lightened your load.

Bibliography

Bercovitch, Sacvan. *The American Jeremiad*. Madison: University of Wisconsin Press, 2012.

brown, adrienne maree. *Emergent Strategy*. Chico, CA: AK Press, 2017.

Brown, Brené. *Braving the Wilderness: The Quest for True Belonging and the Courage to Stand Alone*. New York: Random House, 2019.

Chesterton, Gilbert K., and David Dooley. *The Collected Works of G.K. Chesterton / Heretics. Orthodoxy U.a. / with Introd. and Notes by David Dooley*. San Francisco, CA: Ignatius, 1986.

Deleuze, Gilles, Guattari Félix, and Brian Massumi. *A Thousand Plateaus*. London: Bloomsbury, 2013.

Jennings, Willie James. *Acts (TCB)*. Westminster John Knox, 2017.

———. *The Christian Imagination: Theology and the Origins of Race*. New Haven, CT: Yale University Press, 2011.

Johnson, Paul E. *A Shopkeeper's Millennium: Society and Revivals in Rochester, New York 1815–1837*. New York: Hill and Wang, 2004.

Jüngel, Eberhard. *The Doctrine of the Trinity: God's Being Is in Becoming*. Edinburgh: Scottish Academic, 1976.

Lacan, Jacques, and Bruce Fink. *Ecrits: a Selection*. New York: W.W. Norton & Co., 2004.

Moltmann, Jürgen. *The Crucified God*. Minneapolis, MN: Fortress, 2015.

Schaeffer, Francis A. *How Should We Then Live?*. Old Tappan, NJ: F.H. Revell Co., 1976.

Shellnutt, Daniel and Silliman, Kate. "Ravi Zacharias Hid Hundreds of Pictures of Women, Abuse During Massages, and a Rape Allegation." News & Reporting. Christianity Today, February 11, 2021. https://www.christianitytoday.com/news/2021/february/ravi-zacharias-rzim-investigation-sexual-abuse-sexting-rape.html.

Smith, James K. A. *Desiring the Kingdom: Worship, Worldview, and Cultural Formation*. Grand Rapids, MI: Baker Academic, 2011.

Winnicott, Donald W. "Fear of Breakdown." *British Psychoanalysis*, 2017, 121–130. https://doi.org/10.4324/9781351262880-11.

Zacharias, Ravi K., and Norman L. Geisler. *Is Your Church Ready?: Motivating Leaders to Live an Apologetic Life*. Grand Rapids, MI: Zondervan, 2010.

www.ingramcontent.com/pod-product-compliance
Lightning Source LLC
Chambersburg PA
CBHW051658090426
42736CB00013B/2437